Law and Disorder

"Your Honor, I decline to answer on the grounds of self-incarceration."

Law and Disorder

Absurdly Funny Moments
from the Courts

CHARLES M. SEVILLA

Illustrations by Lee Lorenz

W. W. NORTON & COMPANY

New York   London

For information about permission to reproduce selections from this book,
write to Permissions, W. W. Norton & Company, Inc.,
500 Fifth Avenue, New York, NY 10110

For information about special discounts for bulk
purchases, please contact W. W. Norton Special Sales at
specialsales@wwnorton.com or 800-233-4830

Manufacturing by Courier Westford
Book design by Ellen Cipriano
Production manager: Louise Parasmo

Library Of Congress
Cataloging-in-Publication Data

Sevilla, Charles M., author.
Law and disorder : absurdly funny moments from the courts /
Charles M. Sevilla ; illustrations by Lee Lorenz
pages cm
ISBN 978-0-393-34953-5 (pbk.)
1. Law—United States—Anecdotes. I. Lorenz, Lee, illustrator. II. Title
K184.S484 2014
349 7302'07—dc23
2014001249

W. W. Norton & Company, Inc.,
500 Fifth Avenue, New York, N.Y. 10110
www.wwnorton.com

W. W. Norton & Company Ltd., Castle House,
75/76 Wells Street, London W1T 3QT
1 2 3 4 5 6 7 8 9 0

One of the Seven [wise men of Greece]
was wont to say: That laws were like cobwebs,
where the small flies are caught and
the great break through.

—Sir Francis Bacon

Contents

"Begging Your Honor's pardon, but isn't life
plus a thousand years a little harsh?"

Introduction

For most of my legal career, I have sought redemption in writing satiric novels and humor anthologies. Writing has been my therapy, humor my cheery companion. Have a problem? Laugh at it, laugh with it, and most important, laugh at yourself. Surely, as Mark Twain said, "Against the assault of laughter nothing can stand." I've spent a lot of time off my feet.

Most people don't think of the law as a fertile source of humor. If they are consumers of what the law offers in the courts, their experiences are either a painful ordeal or something in which survival is a victory. But even in the courts, humor pops up unexpectedly. When it does, for many years my friends have been sending me these memorialized moments in transcript form. I share them with others hungry for a morsel of levity in magazine columns pompously titled "Great Moments in Courtroom History."

These are "Great Moments." They are "great" only because they are different from the humdrum of normal courtroom fare; they are "moments" in the sense of unique instants of time. Put together, they are significant in the sense that the first voyage of the *Titanic* was notable to navigation.

. . .

As with the last two books, *Disorderly Conduct* (Norton, 1987, by Uelmen, Jones, and yours truly) and *Disorder in the Court* (Norton, 1992, yours truly again), the reader will find the humor sophomoric, scatological, very profane, and overtly sexual in content. In other words, just the sort of thing my readers love. But it's not my fault. This is the argot of the twenty-first-century American criminal courts.

Many judges have noted and lamented the decline in language usage in the criminal justice system. It's obvious. The highway robber of old accosted his fellow traveler with the clearly stated demand: "Stand and deliver." Now, it's just a mouthful of profanity peppered with ubiquitous four-letters word commencing with an "f." As one justice rued, "Not everyone can be an F. E. Smith (later Earl of Birkenhead) who, in his speech in 1920 in the House of Commons on the Matrimonial Causes Act, referred to it [intercourse] as 'that bond by which nature in its ingenious telepathy has contrived to secure and render agreeable the perpetuation of the species.'" *People v. Callahan*, 168 Cal.App.3d 631, 635 n. 7 (1985). Ah, those were the days.

But such is not today's reality. Consider this nasty exchange from a Maryland proceeding:

> THE COURT Give me the file back. He might be under contempt of court. Now, stand up there. Come back to that table there. Step on up now. What's wrong with you?
>
> MR. JOHNSON What the fuck you think wrong with me, man? Goddamn, I'm trying to tell you I ain't have no mother fucking option in this shit, man.
>
> THE COURT All right.
>
> MR. JOHNSON What the fuck? You think everybody just want to go sit in prison for the rest of their life because

you ain't got nothing better to do than to sit up there and crack jokes. This ain't no mother fucking joke, man. This is about my goddamn life.

THE COURT That cost you five months and twenty-nine days in addition to the three years I've just given you. *[Contempt number 1]*

MR. JOHNSON Fuck this shit, man.

THE COURT All right. That's five months and twenty-nine more in addition to the five months and twenty-nine I've given you. *[number 2]*

MR. JOHNSON Fuck you, bitch.

THE COURT That makes ten months plus the ten, twenty-nine days. That's twelve months. That's a year. Call me that again and I'll give you another one.

MR. JOHNSON Fuck you, bitch.

THE COURT That's five months and twenty-nine days. That's three years. That's five months and twenty-nine days. . . . That's consecutive to the three years that you're now doing. Each one of those. Separate and independent. *[number 3]*

MR. JOHNSON If I had a gun, your mother fucking head would be splattered all over the back of the goddamn wall for—

THE COURT And you'd better shoot straight when you try. When you get out come on. Five months and twenty-nine more for that. . . . *[number 4]*

MR. JOHNSON Whatever, man. You're tired of giving it out? Did you finish or what?

THE COURT Well, we can see. That's five months and twenty-nine more. *[number 5]*

MR. JOHNSON Kiss my ass again.

THE COURT Five months and twenty-nine more. *[number 6]*

MR. JOHNSON Kiss my ass again until you're tired of giving me another.

THE COURT That's six of them.

MR. JOHNSON Kiss my ass again.

THE COURT Seven. Five months and twenty-nine days. *[number 7]*

MR. JOHNSON Fuck you. Kiss my ass again.

THE COURT Five months and twenty-nine days. *[number 8]* . . . Consecutive. . . .

MR. JOHNSON So, you finished giving out time?

THE COURT I guess. Until you cuss again.

MR. JOHNSON Suck my dick.

THE COURT Five months and twenty-nine days consecutive. *[number 9].* . . .

MR. JOHNSON You finished?

THE COURT I suppose.

MR. JOHNSON Well, what the fuck are you holding me for then?

THE COURT Five months and twenty-nine more days. Consecutive. *[number 10]*

MR. JOHNSON Get the fuck off me, man.

THE COURT Call the next one . . . if I'd have had a shotgun I need to have shot him but I don't have it today. Call the next case.

That gem comes from *Johnson v. State*, 642 A.2d 259, 261–262 (Md.App. 1994) and was called to my attention by Brian D. Shefferman of Rockville, Maryland. I don't know what is more deplorable, the defendant's profane language or the judge's provocations and piling up nearly six years of time on Johnson as if he were stacking a pile of pennies. You'll be happy to know the Court of Appeal reversed all the contempts.

I must thank all my contributors, many of whose names you will see frequently associated with the following contributions. If they are from California, I only cite the city location. All Seventh Circuit quotes are courtesy of former Federal Defender Richard Parsons, who authored the newsletter entitled *The Back Bencher* and contributed many appellate court gems.

I also would acknowledge and extend great thanks to W. W. Norton & Company and particularly to Amy Cherry and Anna Mageras for bringing this book to life. Thanks to Joe Vallely, my agent, and my wife, Donna, for their inestimable contributions. Finally, many thanks to the lawyers and staff at the California Attorneys for Criminal Justice, and particularly to the folks who put their magazine, *Forum*, together. They have been publishing these snipets in my column, "Great Moments in Courtroom History," for the last thirty-five years.

Lastly, I heartily thank the happy lawyer courtroom warriors who daily do battle in the front lines defending their clients' rights. Carry on!

Law and Disorder

"Your Honor—my client requests a change of venue."

{ 1 }

The Defendants

May a person who enters the habitat of another at 3 o'clock in the morning for the announced purpose of killing him, and who commences to beat the startled sleeper's bed with a stick and set fires under him, be entitled to use deadly force in self defense after the intended victim shoots him in the back with an arrow? Upon the basis of these bizarre facts, we hold that he may not, and instead, must suffer the slings and arrows of outrageous fortune (with apologies to William Shakespeare and *Hamlet*, Act III, sc. 1).

PEOPLE V. GLEGHORN, 193 CAL.APP.3D 196, 198–99 (1987)

I remember the time that I was kidnapped and they sent a piece of my finger to my father. He said he wanted more proof.

RODNEY DANGERFIELD

Another Case of Mistaken Identification

(Kenneth Quigley, San Francisco)

DEFENDANT I'm representing myself because my attorney stole my DNA and cloned me into a male dog. I'm not dealing with him anymore.

THE COURT *[to clerk]* Who is next on appointed counsel conflict's list?

DEFENDANT I'm not dealing with no man. If it's not a lady, I'm representing myself. And I can prove to the Court the charges they got me for wasn't me. It was my clone, and I'm going to prove that to the Court. I'm tired of them violating me. Every time my clone does something, they're charging me with it.

True Romance

(Gregory B. English, Alexandria, VA)

Q. Were you involved in a romantic relationship with her?
A. I ain't involved in no romantic relationship with her. I'm married to her.

A Very Dangerous Question

(Hon. David L. Piester, Lincoln, NE)

THE COURT Mr. Defendant, your affidavit is not complete, so I must ask you the questions you didn't answer on the form. First, what is your marital status?
A. *[Long pause]* Adequate.

Negative Pregnant

(Jay Jaffe, Beverly Hills)

In a paternity action, the blood test having conclusively proven that he was the father of the child, Mr. Smith testified that he could not possibly be the father of the child since he did not have continuous access to the mother. When asked by the judge to describe his relationship with the mother, Mr. Smith replied, "On again, off again."

Federal Indictment Excerpt

(Steve Cron, Santa Monica)

At approximately 9:00 a.m., the three defendants entered a Coldwell Banker office in Hacienda Heights, California, and attempted to commit a bank robbery. Upon learning that Coldwell Banker is not a bank, the three defendants left the premises and drove away looking for a bank to rob.

Parole Hearing Conduct Report

(Kevin McCoy, Anchorage, AL)

The following is his institutional summary: Fifteen disciplinary actions, two for fighting, others for jamming a locking device, mutilating a T-shirt, threatening an officer, hitting a civilian during a basketball game, yelling, lying. . . . Additionally, he impregnated a prisoner while in the sex offender treatment program. On the positive side . . . he has a certificate for exemplary umpire duties in the softball league.

Second Noblest Profession

(Thomas C. Carter, Alexandria, VA)

The defendant said that prior to the occurrence of the instant offense, he hoped to attend medical school and become a physician. However, he said he believes that with a felony conviction, he will be precluded from achieving this goal. He added that he is now considering becoming a lawyer.

Sorry, Can't Make the Probation Interview

(Jeremy Warren, San Diego)

[From a Probation Report] Approximately two or three days prior to our scheduled meeting with his attorney in my office. He was basically telling me that he was too busy to come to the office. He wasn't going to make it. He didn't have any, quote, jack-off time. He had used up all his jack-off time; and that's exactly what this was about. It was just jack-off time and he didn't have any time to do that. After he had discussed the fact that he wasn't coming to the meeting, he directed me to tell his attorney that the attorney and I can come down to his shop, and bring him lunch. He directed me to go to Subway, that he didn't eat pork, that I was to bring him a sandwich and he went on to discuss all of the condiments that could be put on the sandwich, including extra pickles.

Search and Seizure

(Sam Polverino, Santa Clara)

Q. At that point is it your testimony that she reached in with her left hand, inside of your pants?

A. She was fondling me, you know. We were playing, you know. We were goofing around. She was fondling me and it took her a little while, but she found it.

THE COURT Would you clarify that, please? Found what?

A. Found the wallet.

Rear-Guard Motion

(Jim Thompson, Berkeley)

On April 5, 1996, this court ordered plaintiff to show cause why this court should not impose . . . sanctions upon him for filing a motion for improper purposes. The motion which plaintiff filed was entitled "Motion to Kiss my Ass" . . . in which he moved "all Americans at large and one corrupt judge Smith [to] kiss my got [sic] damn ass you sorry mother fucker."

[Washington v. Alaimo, 934 F.Supp. 1395 (1996)]

Long Gun

(Carl Hancock, San Diego)

Q. Do you want to testify?

A. I don't want to be involved.

Q. You'd just rather not be here?

A. I'd rather not be here.

Q. But you're here, is that correct?

A. Yes, I am.

Q. You've heard the testimony that on July 4th, you had a sawed-off .12-gauge shotgun down your sweats. Again, is there anything you can think of that could possibly even be mistaken for something like that?

A. No, unless . . . my penis.

Moonstruck

(Michele Yamaki, Los Angeles)

Minute order: The Court trial resumes with defendant and counsel present as heretofore. Court trial is held. People waive opening statement. Defendant removes his pants, exhibits his backside, and makes statements to the Court. Defendant's response is deemed a waiver of opening statement.

Yellow Press

(Charles Feer, Bakersfield)

The victim said the next morning when she awoke, she was late for work. She said she got up to iron some clothing and noticed there was a strange color coming from the steam iron. She asked the suspect if he had done something to the iron and he said he had urinated in it.

Statement in Mitigation

(Delgado Smith, Texarkana, TX)

DEFENSE COUNSEL I think if anything is true, it is that this man, the defendant, through his lifetime, has suffered from an incurable kind of kindness in which, for whatever reason, his mother and his father sought to protect him in every way that they knew how. I can tell you that I have never seen a weaker human being than this man. This man is the biggest wimp I have ever seen in my life. He cowers over in the corner of his cell. The people there come and steal his food. They pee on him and laugh. If he were prettier, he'd be somebody's girlfriend. This man is a weak man.

Bright Shining Thug

(Russ Stetler, San Francisco)

COUNSEL Well, briefly, my client has talked to three separate people in the probation department, probation never being notable for their charity, and all three of those people, all conclude that as far as criminals go, my client is a pretty good candidate.

THE COURT Yeah, beats up old ladies.

DA The only thing I'd add is in reference to his statement to the probation officer that he was with a bunch of friends and they were doing it, a police officer observed the struggle and observed him throw the woman down, and there is no mention of seeing any other people anywhere in the area.

COUNSEL I don't think he's trying to suggest someone else did this crime. I think he's talking about his friends on the street.

THE COURT Yeah, he's talking about a bunch of guys who say, "You ought to go out and rob old ladies, beat them up, take their chains away from them, and run." That's what he did. He's a coward, he's a thief, and he's a lot of other things.

COUNSEL He's a thief.

THE COURT He's a coward. He hit a seventy-four-year-old lady, knocked her on her back, and he took her chain.

COUNSEL He's not proud of it, Judge.

THE COURT He's not batting an eye. He's not batting an eye. You got anything to say for yourself?

DEFENDANT Yeah, I'm sorry,

THE COURT What's that?

DEFENDANT I'm sorry it happened.

THE COURT You're sorry you're in jail, aren't you?

DEFENDANT Yeah.

THE COURT He's not exactly a shining example for American youth.

COUNSEL That's why we pleaded him guilty.

"If I Wanted to Listen to an Ass——"

(Jacqueline Crowle, San Diego)

THE COURT For the record, you can, of course, by acting out be found guilty of contempt and punished for contempt regardless of what happens in these cases. There's always the chance of appeal. There is an automatic appeal.

DEFENDANT I'm going to get life in prison and you're going to put a contempt on top of it. Oh! Oh! Oh!

THE COURT I'm telling you there could be an appeal in these cases.

DEFENDANT That's bullshit.

THE COURT Listen to what I'm saying.

DEFENDANT I'm not listening to a shit. I didn't want to come over here. If I wanted to listen to an asshole, I'd go take a shit.

The Mouth

(Robert Spertus, Berkeley)

THE COURT This is your opportunity, sir, to tell me why I should relieve not only your lawyer but his entire office, the Public Defender's Office in this case. Go right ahead, sir.

DEFENDANT If he's my mouthpiece and my mouth ain't saying what my brain wants it to say, then something is out of order, and it is just not working.

Good Penmanship

(Luke & Marti Hiken, San Francisco)

DEFENDANT I want to stand in pro per. That is my right and I want to be in pro per. I don't want this man to defend me.

THE COURT Well, all he's trying to do right at the moment is to see to it that you get a fair hearing.

DEFENDANT Hey, man, I can send myself to the pen just as good as he can.

The Good Samaritan

(Gary Nelson, San Diego)

Q. You just happened to be wandering out in the projects at five-thirty, and just happened to see those two people at the porch?

A. Yes.

Q. And just happened to decide to get a piece of cardboard to shove it through the slot?

A. Yes.

Q. You didn't know if they wanted to get the gas in the slot?

A. They kept trying for a while, and I was watching.

Q. Are you the one that said, "Don't pour it on the door, let me make this cardboard so you can get inside"?

A. No, I didn't say that.

Q. Why'd you join them at all?

A. Well, I knew the people.

Q. So what? You know a lot of people in the projects, right?

A. Yes.

Q. You see people in the projects, you know, robbing somebody, you go up and help them rob?

A. Yes.

Q. You see people in the projects beating up somebody, and you go and help them?

A. Yes.

Q. You see people in the projects shooting somebody, and you pull out your piece and get off a few rounds yourself?

A. Yes.

Q. You are just a real helpful person, right, and you couldn't stop yourself from helping other people you see in the projects?

A. I can stop myself.

Q. You didn't stop yourself that night.

A. No, not that night.

Q. And you're telling the jury your motivation was you are just a helpful person?

A. I was helpful, yes.

A Man of Few Words

(Mark Arnold, Bakersfield)

THE COURT Sir, are you Dan ——

DEFENDANT Fuck you.

THE COURT —— Junior?

DEFENDANT Fuck you.

THE COURT Show the defendant is present and in custody.

COUNSEL I reviewed the report and it appears that he pled guilty.

DEFENDANT Fuck you.

THE COURT He doesn't like you either.

DEFENDANT Fuck you.

Going to Disneyland?

(Earl Bute, New York City)

Q. If this person was traveling at breakneck speed at you, how come he didn't get all the way over to you?

A. Because that is nowhere. He's riding kamikaze at somebody's car. And why wasn't he at Disneyland, shithead?

Defendant Says

(Jack Campbell, Vista)

[From a probation report on a gang member convicted of robbery]
The defendant's attitude toward law enforcement is best expressed
in his own words: "The only good cop is a dead cop. And there
aren't enough good cops."

Pro Per At-Large

(Michael Shannon, Pasadena)

A. With the DA:

DEFENDANT Your Honor, may I state one more thing? When
I was here the last time, I would like to state for the record
that I'm going to file a motion to dismiss the DA from the
case because me and him as you left us here to speak alone
here, he was very derogatory.

DA I wanted to make sure you didn't steal anything from the
court file.

B. With the Court:

DEFENDANT Your Honor, may I ask you a question? With all
due respect, sir. Who runs your courtroom, the DA or
you?

THE COURT I do.

DEFENDANT Because if the DA runs your courtroom, with
all due respect, you're in the wrong seat.

Understanding Parents

(Richard Berman, Fresno)

[From a probation report] According to the police department report, the minor sold marijuana to another student at his school. The minor stated that he had also sold marijuana in the past. A search of the minor's room revealed that the minor was growing the marijuana in his bathroom after telling his parents it was a "science experiment."

Defendant in the Spin Zone

(Charles Bonneau, Sacramento)

Q. Basically, out of all your criminal convictions, you're pretty much denying responsibility for all of them, aren't you?

A. No.

Q. You're not? You had an excuse for Joanne, right?

A. An excuse?

Q. Yes. Aren't you basically saying it's really Joanne's fault, Joanne is the one who is violent in the relationship?

A. Joanne did start that fight, yes.

Q. Okay. So you're really denying responsibility for that?

A. No. It takes two to tango, and I did fight back.

Q. Okay. And the receiving stolen property, you're mitigating that, right?

A. I had somebody bring over a safe for me to open. I had no idea that it was stolen.

Two Views of a Robbery

(Marcia Levine, Auburn)

[Witness View]

A. And while I was eating, I heard a shot. I saw this black guy holding a gun, pacing the counter. I think he was also ordering something to eat.

Q. You testified it was a medium gun. Today you testified it's a small gun.

A. Well, when the robbery happened, I remember it was a small gun.

Q At the preliminary hearing you testified it was a medium gun?

A Well, I really meant a large one, but a small size.

[Defendant's View]

Q. What happened when you went to Der Wienerschnitzel?

A. I was going to place an order. The lady asked me for my order, and for some reason I just jumped to the window, and I told her to give me the money and she didn't give me the money so I had a knife and told her to give me the money and she didn't give it to me and I wasn't going to hurt her, but I just tried to scare her and she took off running, so I unplugged the cash register and I ran out of the place with it.

Q. Had you planned to do that when you went up to the Der
   Wienerschnitzel?

A. No, I never plan things like that. I don't do things like that
   very often.

Not That Kind of Guy

(Richard Krech, Oakland)

Q. And had you ever argued with her about her father?

A. Yeah. One day when she was drunk, she accidentally told
   me that her dad was the one who shot me, but I don't
   know if she said it out of playing or because she was under
   beer. We were high, and she just spit it out.

Q. And was your relationship good or bad with her father?

A. It wasn't really that good because they never really liked
   me because I'm not rich like them. I'm not high class.
   Like, they expected her to get a guy with high class. I'm
   not that kind of guy.

Non-Commie Prison Bound

(Mark Arnold, Bakersfield)

Q. You want to go back to prison, did you say?

A. Yes.

Q. Well, now, you understand that the judge at the time of
   sentencing will choose either the lower or the middle or
   the upper term?

A. Yes sir.

Q. And you understand that if you are not a citizen you could be deported?

A. I am not a communist.

Mideast Justice

(Paul Potter, Pasadena)

The Probation Officer received court documentation from defense counsel and the defendant's Alien File (A-File) that were translated into English from Farsi. It appears that on February 9, the defendant was scheduled to be punished by the Administrative Justice, Islamic Republic of Iran for committing the crimes of "Enmity with the God" and "Scum of the Earth." According to Section 3, Article 90, of the Penal Code, punishment for Enmity with the God and Scum of the Earth is one of the following: killing, execution, amputation of right hand and left leg, or exiling from the town.

Felony Dumb?

(Richard Krech, Oakland)

DA And lastly, Your Honor, I already explained the strike consequences of these charges; however, if in the future they are all considered serious felonies under the law and if in the future the defendant was convicted of a serious felony, not only would this strike require twenty-five years to life be imposed but the Court would be required by law to impose an additional five years as a result of this guilty plea to that twenty-five to life.

THE COURT Yes, that is correct. And do you also understand that, Mr. Defendant?

A. Yes. I mean I'm doing seventeen years, what do you think I'm going to do after I spend seventeen years in prison. You think I'm going to do something stupid?

THE COURT Well, it's possible.

Pro Per Complaint

(Jeremy Warren, San Diego)

The government may say petitioner's counsel is an F. Lee Bailey, but this Honorable Court with an impartial examination of the issues raised may be excused if it reaches the conclusion that petitioner received the services of Barnum and Bailey instead of F. Lee Bailey. . . . The government attempts *reductio ad absurdum* and tries to transmute base metal into gold.

Voluntary Plea Questioned

(Libby Pace, Los Angeles)

THE COURT Have any other promises been made to you, or have any threats been made against you or members of your family to get you to enter into this plea agreement today?

DEFENDANT No threats. Just that . . . No, no threats.

THE COURT Any other things done to your family?

DEFENDANT Yeah.

[DEFENSE COUNSEL] The Court indicated it would be disposed to marry him.

THE COURT That is not a threat.

Gangsters at Work

(John Kucera, Redding)

DEFENDANT This is racism to the utmost. I asked for all my witnesses. My witnesses haven't been here or nothing. I'm not prepared to go to trial.

DA May the record please reflect that the prosecutor on this case is also African-American.

DEFENDANT That don't mean nothing. He ain't no African-American.

THE COURT He looks like one to me.

DEFENDANT He ain't no damn African-American. He's a Uncle Tom. I've got prosecution misconduct on him. I got him on tape claiming gang-banging accusations to me telling me he's a Cripp from Long Beach and I'm a Blood. I can not go to trial with this guy at all. I'm a Blood, and he's a Cripp. We're known enemies. I cannot go to trial with him. I have that on tape. I would like to have that on tape.

Under Oath

(Michael Chaney, Los Angeles)

Q. Do you understand that you're under oath?
A. Yes.
Q. What does under oath mean to you?
A. That I'm under eighteen.

An Innocent Question

(John Aquilina, Riverside)

[Man approaches Counsel in hallway]

MAN Do you know where I go for a battery?

COUNSEL A court case as opposed to something for your car?

MAN Yeah.

COUNSEL Are you a witness, victim, or defendant?

MAN No, I'm the guy who did it.

One-Note Charlie

(Michael Chaney, Los Angeles)

Q. You have the right to remain silent. Do you understand?

A. Bitch.

Q. Anything you say may be used against you in court. Do you understand?

A. Bitch.

Q. You have the right to the presence of an attorney before and during any questioning. Do you understand?

A. I'm rich, Bitch.

Q. If you cannot afford an attorney, one will be appointed for you, free of charge, before any questioning, if you want. Do you understand?

A. Bitch.

Q. Do you want to talk about what happened?

A. Bitch. I understand my rights, Bitch!

The Human Lie Detector

(Ed Schulman, Northridge)

DA I believe that you also testified that her mom confirmed her name and her date of birth?

DEFENDANT No. She confirmed that she was eighteen when her daughter had told me she was eighteen the second time I met them, when she introduced me to her daughter.

DA You heard her mom testify that she never introduced you to her daughter?

DEFENDANT Anybody could lie.

DA You're claiming she lied?

DEFENDANT Yes.

DA Would it be fair to say that Angelica was lying too?

DEFENDANT Yes.

DA And Judith is lying?

DEFENDANT Yes.

DA And Laura is lying?

DEFENDANT Yes.

DA What about the neighbor, Mr. L., who saw you approach his girlfriend in an assertive manner, is he lying too?

DEFENDANT Yes.

DA And Pedro, he's lying too?

DEFENDANT Yes.

DA Did I leave anybody out?

DEFENDANT You forgot yourself.

The Great Bank Robbery

(Richard J. Krech, Oakland)

DEFENDANT Yeah, he hide in the back and then we turn the corner and once we got on the freeway, he got in the front seat and said that that was all he had.

Q. How much did he have?

A. He showed me two stacks of ones. A hundred dollars in each stack. He gave me a hundred and fifty and that didn't seem right to me that he gave me a hundred and fifty dollars.

Q. Okay. So, he gave you a hundred and fifty dollars for driving.

A. Um-hmm.

Q. So, you really don't know how much he got out of there with. Did he say anything about how it went down or how things went in the bank?

A. He said the robbery note was messed up. He said the note was messed up and instead of asking for hundreds and fifties, they asked for ones and fifties.

Q. Left off a few zeros or something?

A. Yeah.

Q. America's Funniest Video here at the bank.

Assaulting an Angel

(Dennis Roberts, Oakland)

In *People v. Murdoch*, 194 Cal.App.4th 230 (2011), the Court granted Murdoch's motion for self-representation. Murdoch informed the Court his defense to the assault charges was that the victim was not human, as indicated by the fact he lacked shoulder blades which are "symbolic of angelic beings." To demonstrate his defense, Murdoch asked a victim: "Can you shrug your shoulders like this?" The victim could do so. Murdoch announced that the prosecution had an "imposter" in court.

Culinary Prison Education

(Jodea Foster, Chico)

Q. You're going to have to help the jury out. Do inmates at the jail kind of talk about committing crime all the time while they're in jail?

A. Well, going to jail is just kind of like going to a preschool, a high school for criminals. Going to prison is kind of like a college.

Q. Okay.

A. You got fifty inmates that are all criminals there. What do you think the main topic of conversation is?

Q. Crime?

A. Correct.

Q. When they talk about committing crime, they talk about how to commit crime?

A. I've learned more inside jail about committing crimes than I have learned outside.

Q. So they talk about how to commit crimes?

A. Yes.

Q. And do they use examples when they talk about how to commit crimes?

A. If you want, you can get a diagram as long as you eat it afterwards.

Loose Lips

(Martin Buchanan, San Diego)

[http://www.legal-forms-kit.com/legal-jokes/stupid-criminals.html]

The defendant was on trial for the armed robbery of a convenience store in a district court when he fired his lawyer. The prosecutor reported that the defendant was doing a fair job of defending himself until the store manager testified that he was the robber whereupon he jumped up, accused the woman of lying, and said, "I should of blown your [expletive] head off." The defendant paused, then quickly added, "if I'd been the one that was there." The jury took twenty minutes to convict and recommended a thirty-year sentence.

Defendant's Notice of Appeal

[http://raymondpward.typepad.com/newlegalwriter/
filed in the U.S. District Court, Western Div. of Wa.]

"I hereby am informing you that I am appealing the asshole decision of Judge [ ] in this matter. You have been hereby served notice. You're not getting away this shit that easy. Signed [defendant]."

Bail Question About Freedom's Rent

(Tom Acorn, Indianapolis, IN)

JUDGE Do you have any questions?

DEFENDANT Yes, Judge, you said I was presumed innocent, right?

JUDGE Yes, that's right.

DEFENDANT Then, what am I doing in jail?

Digital Identification

(Bart Sheela III, San Diego)

Q. Do you recognize the driver of that vehicle in court?

A. Yes, I do.

Q. Could you point and identify where he is sitting and something he is wearing.

A. The defendant is sitting right there waving his middle finger at me in a blue smock.

"Most blatant attempt to suborn a jury I've ever seen."

{ 2 }

The Lawyers

[The lawyers were] mistily engaged in one of the ten thousand stages of an endless cause, tripping one another up on slippery precedents, groping knee deep in technicalities, running their goat-hair and horse hair warded heads against walls of words and making the pretence of equity with serious faces as players might.

CHARLES DICKENS, *BLEAK HOUSE*

A cock-brained solicitor, a law puddler, a mere and arrant pettifogger, a pork who never read any philosophy, an unbuttoned fellow, a boar in a vineyard, a snout in pickle . . . the shame of all honest attorneys, an unswilled hogshead, a tradesman of the law, whose best ware is only gibberish, a serving man and solicitor compounded into one mongrel— an apostate scarecrow, a vagabond and ignoramus, a beetle, a daw, a horsefly, a nuisance and bronze ass.

ADAPTED FROM JOHN MILTON'S COLASTERION BY
M. FRANCES MCNAMARA, *2000 FAMOUS LEGAL QUOTATIONS*, P. 373

Capital sans Capital

(Daniel Gunther, San Francisco)

In a two paragraph opinion, the court of appeal affirms the trial court's grant of habeas relief. "We have read the record, read the briefs, and heard oral argument. We are left with the firm conviction that [defendant] Macias was denied his constitutional right to counsel in a capital case in which actual innocence was a close question. The state paid defense counsel $11.84 per hour. Unfortunately, the justice system got only what it paid for."

[*Martinez-Macias v. Collins*, 979 F.2d 1067 (5th Cir. 1992)]

Why I Was Late with My Motion

(Hon. Kenneth Chotiner, Los Angeles)

Although defense counsel admits fault in not filing the written notice of motion, he points out that the fault is not all his own. It was because he was delayed, missed his client in Riverside, and was arrested and charged as a felon in Chino, resulting in stress and the failure to file the motion papers herein demanded by the People.

Ready for Action

(Timothy Rien, Livermore)

THE COURT Counsel, are you going to be ready on the defendant's case if the People are ready?

COUNSEL That name doesn't ring a bell, but I'm ready. What's the charge?

THE COURT Capital murder.

A Question of Relevance

(Stephen Sadowsky, Los Angeles)

COUNSEL Are you telling the truth?
PROSECUTOR Objection; irrelevant.

The Record Is Long Play

(Harry L. Jacobs, Merced)

DEFENSE COUNSEL Could we go off the record?
THE COURT Yes. *[Off the record]*
THE COURT Back on the record.
COUNSEL I intend to ask for—
DEFENDANT Excuse me, like a movie I seen once; back on the record, off the record. It's driving me crazy. I don't know, you just go off the record, go back on the record.
DISTRICT ATTORNEY It wasn't the movie *Rush to Judgment*, I can tell you that.

Full-Service Objection

(Madeline McDowell, Lompoc)

COUNSEL Though, just in case I forget about it, it's a matter to my way of thinking, that has federal due process implications and the Fifth Amendment to the United States Constitution, the corollary right to a jury trial I think contained within the Fourth Amendment of the United States Constitution and the Code of Hammurabi.

THE COURT You left out the Magna Carta, Counsel.

DEFENSE COUNSEL And the Magna Carta.

Say What?

(J. J. Paul, Indianapolis, IN)

DA Do you know Raymond?

COUNSEL Your Honor, I'm gonna object on this basis, this is certainly outside the scope of the direct examination.

PROSECUTOR Your Honor, these questions are, are preliminary to the manner of for which the questions are designed for relevance and scope.

THE COURT For what?

PROSECUTOR If the Court will allow me to proceed.

THE COURT I'm afraid I don't follow you.

PROSECUTOR Now the question are, the questions are not outside the scope of direct examination Your Honor because it's, they're merely a preliminary foundation questions to direct this witness to the substance of that testimony that was referred to, although not referred to by name.

COUNSEL Same objection, Your Honor.

THE COURT Objection is sustained.

Surgical Strike

(Alex Landon, San Diego)

Plaintiff moves the Court for a continuance of the trial for the reason that counsel for the plaintiff is recovering from dick surgery and because of continuing pain is unable to properly represent the plaintiff in a trial. Counsel is unable to sit for long periods of time.

Like It Is

(Richard J. Krech, Oakland)

COUNSEL Well, Your Honor, I just feel this trial is a travesty. You have done everything you can to hogtie the defense from presenting any evidence on its behalf.

THE COURT Wait a minute. You haven't presented your case yet. You haven't put on any defense yet.

COUNSEL Well, you . . .

THE COURT Wait a minute. Your statement that I prevented you from putting on a defense, you haven't presented your case yet, Counsel. This is the People's case that has been presented, not yours.

COUNSEL Your Honor, good attorneys can present a lot for the defense through the cross-examination of the People's witnesses. The People's witnesses do not exist solely for the purpose of putting on a prosecution case. The People's witnesses also have information in their heads that is useful to the defense. Now, I don't imagine that you've ever done a defense case and I don't want to get into contempt here, but you do not seem to be able to fathom that there are two sides to this case. Now, you may not like the defense side of the case. You seem to have made up your mind about this case in the first ninety seconds in chambers, but I have a job to try and present another side of the case. I think Your Honor forgets the obligation not to make up your mind until all the evidence is in. It's very clear that you've made up your mind about this case. You've got your knife and your fork ready to carve these

folks up and you don't want to hear anything from the
defense. So I ask again for a mistrial.

THE COURT I'll deny your motion for a mistrial.

World's Record

(Howard Price, Beverly Hills)

Q. Do you believe the frequency of bowel movements, five,
fifteen a day as being abnormally high?

A. Yes.

COUNSEL Only a lawyer can ask a question like that.

A. It's for the record.

Rebeat Performance

(Michael J. Oliver, Pleasant Hill)

THE COURT Why should I put him back on the street, only to
have to create a situation where at some point in the future
the officers might have to go out and get him again?

COUNSEL Well, if that situation arises, and it isn't any different than this, it would only consist of my client standing
in the middle of a parking lot, refusing to cooperate with
the officers, and being beaten senseless and taken down
to the jail where he is medically treated.

Nobody Tells Me

(Anne Fragasso, San Diego)

COUNSEL As to the issue about whether my client's representation is compromised, I would tell the Court that the

client has been fully advised and made that decision. That decision was based on my client's interaction with me and the degree of services they perceived they have received so far, and that no one, be it my present supervisor in these cases, will tell me what to do in a case to a point where I act in a way that I feel is contrary to the client's interest. If I was going to be in an office where I was told what to do, then I would become a district attorney. I call my own shots on my own cases for my own clients.

THE COURT I am speechless.

Non-moving Violation

(Jon Bryant Artz, Los Angeles)

COUNSEL Good morning, Your Honor. I am appearing on behalf of my wife.

THE COURT Good morning.

COUNSEL Your Honor, before we go any further in the proceedings, I must inform this Court under the new ethical full disclosure act, I am sleeping with this client.

THE COURT I wish I had the discretion and authority to dismiss this citation. Your client has been punished enough.

Zip It Up

(Jack L. Schwartz, Los Angeles)

DA Judge, you want to clarify one thing? It is my understanding, so it does not come back as a surprise, and that is with respect to the lady's statement that "the defendant took out his penis and asked her to orally copulate him." The defense indicated that it would seek to have the Court exclude that testimony.

THE COURT I would, if it were an issue, I would deem to preclude it as part of your direct examination. Counsel, can you see what cross-examination might cause this issue to rise up?

COUNSEL How can I do that?

DA If you open the door or you open the fly.

Nodding Off

(Daniel A. Horowitz, Oakland)

COUNSEL Your Honor, you were looking at the juror and the DA twice nodded, not just a little bit, big bouncing nods when she is giving the answers that she didn't think she'd do it. And when I yelled out, he just nodded yes to her and smiled. And it's just not proper. It's not accidental.

DA Normally, I don't feel a need to respond. In regard to the juror who just left in this case, Counsel is correct. The first time I nodded, I was making notes of her responses and nodded. The second time, I looked up and the juror smiled and nodded at me. I simply responded and smiled back. I wasn't doing anything inappropriate. I was simply responding.

COUNSEL Your Honor, this is something continuing with the DA. It's voluntary behavior on his part. We're not talking about a nocturnal emission by him. His head gyrates like a trout on a fishhook.

Calling Lazarus

(Charles Feer, Bakersfield)

Q. After you were in the hallway and yelled, police department—you yelled, "Police Department, come out." Is that
correct?

A. I believe that's what I had stated in the report that I said, yes.

Q. Now the reason you said, "Police Department, come out,"
is because you believed that there was someone alive in
that master bedroom. Is that true?

A. No.

Q. You think you were yelling at a dead man to come out of
the bedroom?

Payback Time

(Frank J. O'Connor, Shasta)

WITNESS We haven't talked to anybody. I don't want to do this.

THE COURT I know that. I have been told that.

WITNESS So why are my rights being violated by having to?

THE COURT Your rights aren't being violated.

WITNESS I am being forced to testify against my son's father,
and I don't want to.

THE COURT I understand that. You will be back here on
Tuesday, October 1, at nine o'clock in the morning, and
you're not to talk to anybody out there about this case or
make any scenes out in the lobby. That's all.

WITNESS I'll pay you back *[said on the way out]*.

THE COURT What did she say?

REPORTER: She said, "I will pay you back."

BAILIFF: I think she was referring to the DA, not you, Your Honor.

DA I think she was referring to me.

CLERK: That's what I thought.

COUNSEL Apparently the District Attorney loaned her some money.

Longtime Residents

(Jerry Shuford, Indio)

COUNSEL Sir, may I be heard for the record?

THE COURT You may.

COUNSEL I simply adopt *in haec verba* Mr. M.'s motion except for the name of my client to release on bail. Longtime resident of the community, a man of certain respectability. And I think he should be on the street to help me with the defense. Thank you.

DA Your Honor, both the defendants' rap sheets indicate that they are not only longtime residents of Chino, but also longtime residents of the Chino State Prison.

Ineffective Assistance of Counsel

(Michael Crain, Santa Monica)

[From *Smith v. Ylst*, 826 F.2d 872 (9th Cir. 1987)]

A. The allegation against defense attorney, Mr. D.

D.'s investigator stated that D. smoked marijuana one evening during the course of the trial and that while discussing the case he fluctuated between laughter and stupor. D.'s secretary stated that he told her he was crazy and wanted to go to an insane asylum. D.'s associate said D. accused him of being part of the conspiracy and of trying to take over his practice. D. repeatedly expressed concern that people were going to try to kill him, and came to believe that the original murder was related to an alleged drug smuggling conspiracy involving the victim's relatives and her lover. In addition to the declarations, [the defense] submitted two psychiatric reports in support of the new trial motion. These reports were based on a review of the declarations described above, not on contact with D., and they offered the conclusion that D. exhibited a paranoid psychotic reaction.

B. The Refutation
The prosecuting attorney who conducted the trial offered a declaration saying that D. acted no differently than any other criminal defense attorney.

The Clarification
(Dennis Roberts, Oakland)

THE COURT We're on the record. I did hear the defendant say *chinga tu madre*, which I believe means "motherfucker," and that is what the interpreter did not interpret and I will take appropriate action tomorrow morning.

COUNSEL If I may, Your Honor, to correct your Spanish, I believe it means "fuck your mother" as opposed to "motherfucker."

THE COURT Thank you, sir, that's very helpful.

COUNSEL I knew you wanted that clarification.

In re Resendiz, 71 Cal. App.4th 145 n. 2 (1999)

(Michael Thorman, Hayward)

[Attorney] Basinger begins his declaration as follows: "I am an attorney licensed to practice in the state of California. I have been an attorney for 18 years and have specialize [sic] in criminal defense for the past years." He fails to mention, though, that he was convicted of a felony involving theft in a scheme that victimized his clients and law partners and was disbarred for a substantial part of "the past 18 years." (See *In re Basinger,* 45 Cal.3d 1348 [1988].) In other words, part of the time Basinger was "specializing" involved the study of criminal law from the wrong side of prison bars. One would think an attorney with this history would have at least learned to take some care with documents sworn under penalty of perjury—then again, maybe not.

A Lawyer's Argument

(Barry Schear, San Diego)

Wallace urges his wife was a police agent who coerced him to make admissions. . . . The heart of this assertion of error, that the post-arrest statements should have been suppressed as involuntary (that is, they were coerced), is encapsulated in the following memorable assertion: "If the police had escorted into appellant's holding cell not his wife but rather a boa constrictor, and if after a few minutes in the room with the boa constrictor appellant decided to make a statement, the subsequent statement would clearly be deemed involuntary. There is no basis to distinguish Mrs. Wallace from the boa constrictor."

[*People v. Wallace,* 9 Cal.App.4th 1515, 1520–1521(1992)]

Job Description

(Bill Belden, Indio)

THE COURT The record should reflect we are in chambers. I have, in rather stern words, admonished the Public Defender that to this point I have, in every respect, complied with every request that he has made of me with respect to the calendar, the times of appearances, scheduling of things, to accommodate his office. That, in my opinion, it has been a one-way street. That he has done everything possible to make it difficult for the Court and to not cooperate. And I have asked him to consider his position in that regard because it can be played by two. Is that not in essence what I said?

PUBLIC DEFENDER I wish you would repeat the curse words that you said to me in private, for the record, Your Honor.

THE COURT I said words like damn and hell and things of that sort.

PUBLIC DEFENDER I recall a word beginning with an "f."

THE COURT That's true, too. Is there anything else you want to put on the record?

PUBLIC DEFENDER No, if we're done, I just wanted everything you said to be on the record.

THE COURT All right. It's on the record. I don't know what your point is. What I would urge is that you discuss it with your superiors and see if this is their position to make everything as difficult and time-consuming as possible. Even when you have stipulations as to the nature of substances, you object to what they are. When you know of the officer's qualifications, and have known of it for years, you object, and then we go through it. You, it appears to me, have done everything to make it difficult and impossible.

Final Argument

(Delgado Smith, Texarkana, TX)

THE COURT This is the time for closing argument.

COUNSEL Thank you. Seems like I get up here every time after lunch when we're starting to get drowsy. I am too, so don't feel bad.

THE COURT You're gonna wake them up.

COUNSEL I'm gonna wake you up. This case reminds me of something I read one time. A very prominent lawyer of some repute in the old days, very familiar name, his name is Mr. Abraham Lincoln, stood in front of a jury, just like I am in front of you, very similar case—

THE COURT Automobile collision?

COUNSEL Horse and buggy, I think. Anyway, it was a very similar type—it was an injury case. And he said to the jury—he said, "Let me tell you a story." And he said, "this little girl came running up through the field. Daddy, daddy, daddy." He says, "Yes, my darling? What's the problem?" She says, "Well, the hired hand and the maid, they're down in the barn and—and they're down there again and, well, she's got her dress up and she's taking down her panties and they're right in the middle of the hay and he's taking down his panties and—well, looks like they're gonna pee in the hay again, huh, Dad?"

See, we have the same facts in all of the evidence in this case for both sides, except they came to the wrong conclusion. They're not gonna pee in the hay. The defense came to the wrong conclusion. And they take a conclusion and support it by evidence that is not falsified but can be interpreted in many, many, many ways, albeit only one way, according to them, and that is their way.

Batty Final Argument

(Richard J. Krech, Oakland)

DA Ladies and gentlemen, finally, there has been some popular movies this decade. And when Defense Counsel was talking, I couldn't help but think of some of these popular movies, actually movies based on a series back in the 1960s, *Batman and Robin* series. And that all started with a cartoon book, didn't it? Ladies and gentlemen, like Batman and Robin, this father and son are involved in methamphetamine manufacturing. If you don't believe that Robin knows what Batman's doing or where the Batcave is, where the Batmobile is and Robin doesn't know their next project, he doesn't know how to drive the Batmobile, that's just silly. Batman is a right arm of Robin, is the right arm of Batman. He knows the foes. He knows who the Penguin, the Riddler, Joker, Catwoman is. They're both involved. And the son is, Robin, too, Batman, his dad. Robin doesn't know what Batman is doing? He's more than just on the side. He's actually actively involved. Convict him of both counts.

The Vision

(Delgado Smith, Texarkana, TX)

The victim says she saw double because she was hurt so bad. Instead, she waits a week. She goes in to see a chiropractor referred by her attorney. She was not seeing double. What she saw was dollar signs.

Survival Instinct

(Richard Krech, Oakland)

COUNSEL The People have filed points and authorities for restraining the defendant. With all due respect, I don't believe this is the People's issue, how our client is restrained. It may well be the sheriff's issue. It's clearly the Court's.

PROSECUTOR I believe it's in the People's interest as well.

COUNSEL I don't believe the People have any legitimate interest.

PROSECUTOR I think the People have an interest in the safety of witnesses, particularly the victim, the safety of the people in the courtroom, especially since I'll be here.

Fertile Mind

(Kathy Kahn, San Francisco)

DA Did I hear him say he thinks this may be a case of first impression?

THE COURT I think so.

DEFENSE COUNSEL Yeah.

THE COURT Well, he is very innovative in his motions. It's been my experience that he has a fertile mind and thinks up a lot of issues. Right?

DEFENSE COUNSEL Yes, Your Honor. I only use organic fertilizer.

Full-Service Counsel

(Darryl Mounger, N. Hollywood)

ORDER: The Sheriff is directed to allow the Defense Attorney to cut the defendant's hair while defendant is in Sheriff's lockup.

People v. Avilt (1995)

(Karen Jo Koonan, Oakland)

In a pretrial conference in chambers, the prosecutor, irritated by defendant's smirk, said to defendant something like, "You motherfucker, I'm going to get you." On appeal, the Attorney General suggests there was no misconduct because, by definition, defendant is a "motherfucker," that is, "a person . . . regarded as remarkable, despicable, contemptible or unpleasant." With such an encore, defendant, not surprisingly, contends prejudicial prosecutorial misconduct permeated the trial.

Stamping Out Crime

(Jim Thomson, Berkeley)

Q. Anything else?

A. You know, I can't help but have a moment of comic relief. I used to teach for the National Defense Institute, and our doors were right next to the National District Attorney's College. And one day we put up a schedule for their boot camp, their training program. We said on the third day they went to a chicken farm and learned to crush baby chickens.

PROSECUTOR Yes, we still learn to do that.

Prosecution Insight

(Dan Burland, San Jose)

The People have evidence that the life of the witness Ronnie H. is in jeopardy and it is reasonable to apprehend he will not be able to attend the trial of this matter if he is not alive at that time.

Asinine Argument

(Neil Morse, San Francisco)

COUNSEL What evidence extraneous to that statement exists so that you have some reasonable belief that the confession might not be false? That she's not confessing to a crime that did not in fact occur? And I submit to you that there isn't any. The District Attorney's argument in this case amounts to what I think is proctology.

Question in the Proper Realm

(Mark Arnold, Bakersfield)

Q. Ma'am, isn't it true that you sell your ass for fifteen dollars on the street?

A. No.

DA Objection.

THE COURT Sustain the objection to the form of the question. Let's phrase the questions within the realm of proper court demeanor.

COUNSEL Yes, Your Honor.

THE COURT I would hate to hold you in contempt, but I will if I get another questions phrased in that fashion.

COUNSEL Well, let me rephrase it, Your Honor.

Q. Ma'am, isn't it a fact that on this occasion you went there to sell your ass for fifteen dollars?

Question for a Hostile Witness

(Delgado Smith, Texarkana, TX)

Q. Well, if you want to amplify, ma'am, have you been programmed in some way to say something that might in some way cause this jury to dislike, hate, rogue, despise, or abominate the defendant?

Usual Family (Sopranos?)

(Roland Thnau, New York City)

Q. Did you have a wife?

A. Yes.

Q. Did you have a usual family, a wife, some children, a girlfriend?

A. Yes.

Sex: Paying by the Hour

(David Van Fleet, Chicago)

In an action by the client against her divorce attorney for excessive billing, included was a billing dispute alleging that "legal fees were billed for time during which petitioner and [her attorney] engaged in sexual relations and for personal phone calls to her."

[*In re Marriage of Kantar*, 581 N.E.2d 6, 9 (1991)]

Brevity: The Soul of Wit

(George Schraer, San Diego)

THE COURT Status of the next witness.

COUNSEL Sorry?

THE COURT Length of time?

COUNSEL I'm sorry . . .

THE COURT How long will the testimony be?

COUNSEL Of the next witness? Incredibly short. I don't have any further witnesses lined up for this afternoon.

THE COURT Call your witness.

COUNSEL I'm sorry, I said I don't . . .

THE COURT Call your witness then if it's incredibly short.

COUNSEL That was it.

THE COURT That was it? You don't have any?

COUNSEL Right. I don't have any more. That's why it's so short.

Why People Hate Lawyers

[*In re* S.C., 138 Cal.App.4th 396, 400 (2006)]

This is an appeal run amok . . . Counsel has managed to violate rules of Court; ignore standards of review; misrepresent the record; base arguments on matters not in the record on appeal; fail to support arguments with any meaningful analysis and citation to authority; raise an issue that is not cognizable in an appeal by her client; unjustly challenge the integrity of the opposing party; make a contemptuous attack on the trial judge; and present claims of error in other ways that are contrary to commonsense notions of effective appellate advocacy—for example, gratuitously and wrongly insulting her client's daughter (the minor in this case) by, among other things, stating the girl's developmental disabilities make her "more akin to broccoli" and belittling her complaints of sexual molestation by characterizing them as various "versions of her story, worthy of the Goosebumps series for children, with which to titillate her audience."

Why Clients Love Lawyers

(Michael Ogul, Solano)

THE COURT Let's recall the case.

COUNSEL Hello again everybody.

THE COURT Okay. The defendant is back in court with his counsel. We're in cross-examination. You may resume.

COUNSEL Thank you, Your Honor. I'm just going to wait a second, until my client has a seat.

THE COURT Counsel, I asked you to resume your cross-examination. This isn't a time to shake your client's hand and waste everybody's time who's been sitting here, so proceed.

COUNSEL I'm not wasting anybody's time.

THE COURT Yes, you were, Counsel.

COUNSEL I beg to differ, Your Honor. I think it's quite proper for Counsel to treat their client with respect.

THE COURT Well, you're the only attorney I've ever seen do that every time a client comes out, Counsel, and I've been in this business 28 years. You're unique. You may proceed.

COUNSEL I'm proud to be that way, Your Honor.

Short Witness List

(J. Frank McCabe, San Francisco)

THE COURT Mr. Prosecutor, do you have a short witness?

PROSECUTOR I don't even have a tall witness.

THE COURT Okay, we'll take our evening recess.

Motion to Have Lunch: Granted

(Ephraim Margolin, San Francisco)

Order: Plaintiff's counsel extended a lunch invitation to Defendant's counsel "to have a discussion regarding discovery and other matters." Plaintiff's counsel offered to "pay for lunch." Defendant's counsel failed to respond until the motion was filed.

Defendant's counsel distrusts Plaintiff's counsel's motives and fears that Plaintiff's counsel's purpose is to persuade Defendant's counsel of the lack of merit in the defense case. The Court has no doubt of Defendant's counsel's ability to withstand Plaintiff's counsel's blandishments and to respond sally for sally and barb for barb. Defendant's counsel now makes what may be an illusory acceptance of Plaintiff's counsel's invitation by saying, "We would love to have lunch at Ruth's Chris with/on . . ."

Plaintiff's counsel replies somewhat petulantly, criticizing Defendant's counsel's acceptance of the lunch invitation on the grounds that Defendant's counsel is "now attempting to choose the location" and saying that he "will oblige," but Defendant's counsel "will pay for its own meal."

There are a number of fine restaurants within easy driving distance of both counsels' offices. . . . Counsel may select their own venue or, if unable to agree, shall select from this list in order. The time will be noon during a normal business day. The lunch must be conducted and concluded not later than August 18.

Each side may be represented by no more than two (2) lawyers of its own choosing, but the principal counsel on the pending motions must personally appear. The cost of the lunch will be paid as follows: Total cost will be calculated by the amount of the bill including appetizers, salads, entrees and one non-alcoholic beverage per participant. A twenty percent (20%) tip will be added to the bill (which will include tax). Each side will pay its *pro rata* share according to number of participants. The Court may reapportion the cost on application for good cause or may treat it as a taxable cost.

Thanks for the Case. Now Outta Here!

(Ken Quigley, San Francisco)

THE COURT Sir, you were appointed by me to this case.

COUNSEL That's true.

THE COURT I was looking for a competent attorney. You were walking by. It was between you and Mr. B. I chose you.

COUNSEL I'm sure you won't make that mistake again, Your Honor. In any event, within a week after I was appointed, I filed a challenge to you sitting on this case.

Stipulation

(Russ Robinson, San Diego)

Q. Did he say anything as he laid on the ground?

A. Yes, "What the fuck is this for?"

Q. Was he using any profanities?

COUNSEL I'll stipulate "fuck" is a profanity.

Constitutional English

(Roger Jon Diamond, Santa Monica)

Q. In your mind, was the intent of these performances to sexually arouse the patron and then cause the patron to orgasm?

A. Yes.

COUNSEL Excuse me, "orgasm" is a noun, not a verb. So when you said "to orgasm," you violated a provision of the California Constitution.

THE COURT I don't know that that's in violation . . .

COUNSEL The California Constitution requires that we use English, and to the extent that we don't use proper English, it's a violation of the California Constitution. It's in Article III.

JUDGE Okay. That's enough. Thank you. Let's get on with this.

COUNSEL It's the last witness. I figure I could go out with a flash.

On Lawyers, Fractions, and Quick Thirds

(Bruce Kapsack, Oakland)

Q. The analog would be if I'm driving 60 miles an hour and I drive for three hours, we know I went 180 miles.

A. Essentially.

THE COURT You're going to interject math word problems at that?

COUNSEL Well, we all became lawyers because we didn't want to do math. Except every personal injury lawyer I know can give you a third of a number like that.

Example of My Romantic First

(Paul Grech, Jr., Riverside)

[Prosecutor's argument] So she has intercourse that night. Now, that might not be as romantic as some of our first times. It didn't happen at some high school party where you and the other person were drunk, and you woke up so hungover the next day that you can't remember what you did, who you did it with. It's not that romantic, but it was her first time. She felt comfortable doing this.

Courtroom Technology

(Hugh A. Levine, San Francisco)

THE COURT Show the exhibit.

DA Hard to see. Can we make it more legible?

That's as good as it's going to get.

THE COURT Well, that's not going to work.

DA That's not going to work

THE COURT We do have an Elmo. The question is can I work it?

MADAM CLERK can you help Counsel not break the equipment?

DA I feel like a bull in the china shop.

DEFENSE COUNSEL Don't look at me. The only kind of Elmo I know is the kind that you tickle.

Judge Rules: "Stay Out" Means "Come On In"

(Captain Motion—Michael Kennedy, Victorville)

[From the defense motion] This is being authored on a date that will live in infamy (Pearl Harbor Day) to recount and to address and to grieve a ruling that likewise must live in infamy, if we are further to export to other lands a credible posture of being a nation of laws and not of constabularial and judicial ruffians.

To help the People save their case, in which they themselves had come to realize, and had conceded, that the cops warrantlessly entered defendant's curtilage in their investigatorial foraging, the Court capitalized on its realization that there was a "no trespassing" sign on the back, non-public door and ruled, with a twist, that such really meant "come on in." "Huh?" you say. So did we.

Pertinent facts: these are taken from memory, because the stunning outrage of this matter cannot abide the normal pleading/filing/arraignment formalities: we shall file these pleadings now; the transcript and information filing can trail our presentation. The facts therein are as we state them here.

It was a bright and unstormy night. Armed and purposeful cops went to the house they claim is the defendant's current and active residence, invaded the curtilage surrounding the house (clearly demarked), crept in behind a shed (which is no more than 10 feet both from the door of the attached garage and from the window of the dining area of the residence), only then smelled an odor they associated (in an undefined manner) with methamphetamine manufacturing, and only then heard what they thought was a gunshot (no evidence of one was produced); they then banged on the

door of the attached garage with the "no trespassing" sign embla-
zoned upon it. The garage is an integral part of the residence, and is
so sturdy that it requires aggressive pounding to move open. They
entered the garage. Inside the garage, they observed and searched
and seized the stuff introduced against the defendant at the preliminary hearing, and they arrested everyone. No warrant sup-
ported any part of that invasion (the entry into the curtilage, the
entry into the garage, and the post-entry rummaging throughout
the garage and into its contents and the pockets of its occupants).

The magistrate, conceding that the area entered by the cops was
the curtilage of the defendant's residence, opined, in a ruling surely
to be heard 'round the jurisprudential world, that the placement of
a "no trespassing" sign on the rear garage door (to which there were
no sidewalks, pathways, or any other indicia of general invitation to
the community) was itself an invitation: one would not place a "no
trespassing" sign on the outside of a door inside private areas, went
the "analysis," unless one expects the public to enter into that private area to read the sign, whose language suggests it was placed
there to protect privacy! Uh, Humpty-Dumpty, phone home!

There is no sidewalk leading from any place the police had a
right to be to that garage door area (nor any sign reading "come ye
all in and plunder my privacy, at your will"!) "Well what," one
might desperately pose, "of the magistrate's *ipse dixit* that 'no trespassing' means come on in?" . . . Trespass law "forbids," it does not
invite, intrusions; it recognizes a "right to exclude." That right to
exclude does not concomitantly incorporate a limited privilege of
the excludees to invade to see if they are unwelcome. (Hmm, I suppose a "welcome" mat would then evidence an expectation that no
one would be coming there, because if someone were expected to

come there, they would not have to be "welcomed," is that about right? So, in Victorville "constitution-speak," "no trespassing" means "come on in," and "welcome" means "go away." I get it.)

So, returning from that irrational foray, if it is a given that we have a curtilage (which the DA concedes, as he must), then the expectation of privacy associated with that curtilage is not downgraded by "no trespassing" signs, but is rather elevated. And everyone knows that.

No case is important enough to cause one to lose his soul. The government needs legitimacy much more than it needs yet another block grant notch on its "drug war" big gun; it has plenty of the latter but diminishing quantities of the former. To propose, with a straight face, that this was a lawful search and seizure which could then properly invite criminal prosecution is repugnant to those fundamental elements of human dignity which are supposed to separate man from the lower and unthinking beasts. Every time these games are played by our government, it pushes this republic closer to the abyss. This motion needs to be granted, and we humbly pray that this Court so order.

"The defendant forcibly entered the hen house—in your own words,
what subsequently transpired?"

{ 3 }

The Evidence

We can imagine no reason why, with ordinary care, human toes could not be left out of chewing tobacco, and if toes are found in chewing tobacco, it seems to us that somebody has been very careless.

PILLARS V. R.J. REYNOLDS TOBACCO CO., MISS. 78 SO. 365, 366 (1918)

Truth needs no disguise.

JUSTICE HUGO BLACK IN *HAZEL-ATLAS GLASS CO. V. HARTFORD-EMPIRE CO.*, 322 U.S. 238, 247

The rule of relevance is a necessary concession to the shortness of life.

JUSTICE OLIVER WENDELL HOLMES, JR.

Crack Cocaine

(George Schraer, San Diego)

Q. Where would he hold the cocaine?

A. Between his butt.

Q. At times when he was holding cocaine and selling cocaine, he would put it in his pants?

A. In his butt.

Q. Inside his underwear?

A. No, his ass.

THE COURT I heard of lot of reasons not to smoke cocaine. I just learned another one.

Miranda Ammunition

(Kenneth Cirisan, San Luis Obispo)

Q. Did you advise him of his Miranda rights?

A. Yes, I did. I read them off a card.

Q. Do you have that card with you?

A. Yes, I do.

Q. Could you read the Miranda rights from the card to the jury as you did to the defendant that evening, or should I say, that morning?

A. Yes. The rights I read to the defendant were: "You have a right to remain silent. Anything you say can and will be used against you in a court of law. You have a right to talk to a lawyer and have him present with you while you are being questioned. If you cannot afford to hire a lawyer, one will be appointed to represent you before any shooting, if you wish one."

Good Advice

(Kenneth M. Quigley, San Francisco)

H. reports that he and W. found a large rodent in a rat trap in W.'s apartment. (It was apparent in our visit to the apartment that there were large rodent feces visible on the floor.) H says that he saw W. fondle the feet of the dead rat. H. took the rat and threw it out into the trash receptacle outside. He returned to W.'s apartment the following day and saw a plate in the kitchen with meat on it. The meat was approximately the size and dimension of a rat. He checked the trash receptacle and found no trace of the rat. To this day he believes W. was planning to eat the rat. He advised against accepting any refreshment from W.

Hair-Raising Motion

(Mel Grimes, Pacific Grove)

More time is needed to prepare this case for trial and for the taking of hair samples and lab analysis. The burglar in this case left behind a black cap, which has been examined by a criminalist at the Department of Justice and was found to contain a number of hairs. A search warrant was obtained for the defendant's hair in order to compare it with the hair left on the cap, but when the warrant was served, the defendant had completely shaved his head. More time is necessary in order for the defendant's hair to grow sufficiently to obtain a sample which can be compared to those in the cap. This evidence is necessary because the main issue in the case is the identity of the burglar.

Police Report

(Charles Feer, Bakersfield)

The defendant was transported and booked into the Bakersfield Police Department property room.

Prison Balcony Scene: Romeo and Juliet

(Michael J. Oliver, Pleasant Hill)

A. When I saw Jimmy through the window, he pulled his pants down and was waving his dick at me. And he got called back inside.

Q. By somebody from his side of the module?

A. From one of the other officers.

Q. So other than this kind of nonverbal communication.

A. Yes.

Q. Did you two talk at all?

A. Yes. We said we loved each other.

Gloving Up for Really Dirty Pictures

(Richard Krech, Oakland)

Q. (DA) Officer, did you bring this brown paper bag I'm holding to Court?

A. Yes, I did.

Q. Now, I'm wearing a rubber glove, I'm pulling out of here approximately twenty or thirty pages of magazine pictures. And, Your Honor, Counsel and I will stipulate that what is in those magazine pictures, we don't see any need for it to go to the jury, are depictions of nude adult women in various sexual poses.

Who's Your Sugar Daddy?

(Peter Scalisi, Riverside)

Q. Where are you living?

DA Objection. Irrelevant.

COUNSEL The offer of proof is that the witness will testify the police are paying her rent.

THE COURT You can ask her that.

Q. Who is paying your rent?

A. My sugar daddy.

Q. Who is that?

A. His name is John.

Q. Have the police given you any kind of financial assistance . . . money?

A. No.

Q. Have they provided you with food since your arrest?

A. No.

[*Half hour later*]

Q. Have you received anything in exchange for your testimony this morning?

A. No.

Q. Nothing of any kind?

A. Actually, the police department has furnished me with my room and my food.

Q. About a half hour ago, I asked you the same question and you told the Court, under oath, that it was a sugar daddy who was providing your food and rent.

A. Yes, I know.

Q. Now, were you lying?

A. Yes, I was.

Can't Recall: Ask Fido

(J. Frank McCabe, San Francisco)

Q. Did you talk more about it?

A. I don't remember exactly. I was crying hysterically most of the trip. If I could ask my dog she'd tell you.

Ho Ho Ho

(Michael Goodman, Los Angeles)

[*U.S. v. Murphy*, 406 F.3d 85 (7th Cir. 2005)]

On the evening of May 29, 2003, Hayden was smoking crack with three other folks at a trailer park home on Chain of Rocks Road in Granite City, Illinois. Murphy, Sr., who had sold drugs to Hayden several years earlier, showed up later that night. He was friendly at first, but he soon called Hayden a "snitch bitch hoe."

The trial transcript quotes Ms. Hayden as saying Murphy called her a snitch bitch "hoe." A "hoe," of course, is a tool used for weeding and gardening. We think the court reporter, unfamiliar with rap music (perhaps thankfully so), misunderstood Hayden's response. We have taken the liberty of changing "hoe" to "ho," a staple of rap music vernacular as, for example, when Ludacris raps, "You doin' ho activities with ho tendencies."

Put the Mustard on the Dog

(Don Wager, Los Angeles)

Q. Well, I'll start with the hot dog stand. Did you have a conversation with him while at the hot dog stand?

A. Yes.

Q. Do you remember what the conversation was?

A. Yes.

Q. What was that?

A. How much is your hot dog?

Q. Did he respond?

A. Yes, he did.

Q. Did you have mayonnaise with your hot dog?

THE COURT Mayonnaise with a hot dog?

A. Yes, Your Honor.

THE COURT You're not telling the truth, or something is awfully wrong.

How Fast? Fahrenheit or Celsius?

(Elie Miller, Los Angeles)

Q. How fast is the car coming as it's coming toward you?

A. Real fast.

Q. Could you give us an estimate if you can?

A. Fifty, sixty, eighty.

Q. Fifty, sixty, eighty miles an hour?

A. He was coming through the parking structure fast. I am not a thermometer so I can't tell you the speed limit.

What's in a Name?

(David Clayton, Hauppauge, NY)

Q. You mentioned a nickname or street name of Pookie. The other nine people involved had street names too?

A. Only one of them that I know of.

Q. Who?

A. Roscoe.

Q. You don't have a street name?

A. No. Oh, yes. Dave Ski.

Q. What about your brother Emmit?

A. Em Ski.

Q. You were a member of the group and they knew your street name but you didn't know theirs. Is that what you're telling us?

A. I know one other street name, but I'd rather not say it.

Q. Who's that?

A. Tony Bates.

Q. You can tell us.

A. They used to call him Master Bates.

THE COURT I could have told you that.

Truth or Die

(John Schuck, Palo Alto)

Q. You raised your hand and swore to tell the truth. Do you understand what that means?

A. Yes.

Q. What does it mean?

A. That means that I am under an oath to tell the truth and I swore to tell the truth under oath.

Q. What happens if you don't tell the truth?

A. If you don't tell the truth, I believe you pretty much go to hell, that's what.

The Oath

(Michael D. Chaney, Los Angeles)

CLERK: Do you solemnly swear that the testimony you are about to give in the cause now pending before this Court shall be the truth, the whole truth, and nothing but the truth, so help you God?

WITNESS Yes, I swear. I'll say anything but the truth, nothing but the truth.

Environmental Crime

(Delgado Smith, Texarkana, TX)

Q. You said that these children at 57th Street were playing?

A. One child was aggressively throwing another child into a trash can that was not for recyclable products.

Sticking to the Point

(Delgado Smith, Texarkana, TX)

THE COURT Did you give defense counsel the finger in the hallway?

WITNESS Who?

THE COURT You know who?

WITNESS That guy right there *[indicating]*?

THE COURT You just did it again. You pointed with your middle finger.

Knock Yourself Out

(Delgado Smith, Texarkana, TX)

Q. Describe what you mean by "unresponsive."

A. He appeared to have lost consciousness.

Q. When we come back from recess, I'm going to ask you to demonstrate that.

THE COURT I don't know if he's going to demonstrate being unconscious or not.

Stupid Questions

(Al & Jackie Menaster, Los Angeles)

Q. Do you recognize it?

A. Yes, it's my chain.

Q. How can you be sure it is yours?

A. Because it has my name written on it.

Q. Pretty good reason.

Enchanting

(Delgado Smith, Texarkana, TX)

WITNESS I'm just nervous

THE COURT Don't be. You're amongst friends.

COUNSEL I can see this is stressful for you. I hope that there's nothing intimidating about being in the courtroom?

THE COURT Oh, absolutely not, right?

WITNESS Oh, not a thing.

THE COURT All you need is a bailiff standing behind you with a . . .

WITNESS I've been OM-ing all morning.

The Worst Thing

(Reed Webb, Temecula)

Q. Isn't it fair to say, based on your experience and your familiarity with the drug community in this valley, that ratting out your supplier, if you are a user, ratting out your supplier is about the worst thing you could do?

A. No, it's not the worst thing you could do.

Q. What is the worse thing you could do?

A. The worse thing you could do?

Q. To your supplier. Yes.

A. Quit using drugs.

Apple of Her Eye

(John Schuck, Palo Alto)

Q. Take a look at the man seated two seats to my left, which is your right.

Do you recognize this man?

A. Yes.

Q. And what is his name?

A. Dimitri.

Q. Do you know him by another name?

A. No. Like another name like how?

Q. Do you call him Dimitri?

A. Yes.

Q. Do you call him any other names?

A. I called him asshole if I was mad at him at home.

THE COURT You called him what?

WITNESS I said, I called him asshole when I was mad at him
    at home.

THE COURT I thought you said apple.

Mickey Mouse Dines at the Meatpacking Plant

[*U.S. v. LaGrou*, 466 F.3d 585, 588 (7th Cir. 2006)]

Although LaGrou usually noted product damage on outgoing bills
of lading to customers, LaGrou did not tell its customers the damage was caused by rodents. Instead, LaGrou's practice was to tell the
customer that the product had been thrown out because of ware-
house damage, such as from torn boxes or forklift mishaps. LaGrou
employees started writing MM (short for "Mickey Mouse") on outgoing bills of lading to differentiate the rodent damage from other
warehouse-related damage. Upon discovering that LaGrou employees were using the MM notation for rodent-damaged product,
Stewart instructed them to stop doing so because he did not want
customers asking what MM meant.

The Tone That Opens Pandora's Box

(Quin Denvir, Sacramento)

THE COURT The inference is that this is a good person, a
    monogamous person, that this person is being molested
    by this horrible defendant and she's virtuous. . . . The truth

is if you're going to present evidence of lax hymenal tone, you open up Pandora's Box. . . . And I can live with a conviction or acquittal since I'm most likely going to max you out if you're convicted. If, in fact, you don't introduce lax hymenal tone, then Pandora's Box will stay closed.

Obstruction of Justice

(Russell Robinson, San Diego)

THE COURT This evidence is coming in anyway. What's the difference?

COUNSEL Because the difference is the Evidence Code. I know it gets in our way.

Who's on First?

(Joel Isaacson, Los Angeles)

Q. So, you don't know anybody who went to any kind of induction ceremony, do you?

A. I don't understand what you're talking about.

Q. You know what induction ceremony is, right?

A. Yes.

Q. They didn't have one for you, did they?

A. No.

Q. You don't know of anyone that had one of those, do you?

A. No. Yeah.

Q. Tim C. had one, didn't he?

A. No.

Q. You talk to him about that?

A. Me?

Q. Yes.

A. Myself?

Q. Yes.

A. I'm not nuts.

Q. No, I said you talked to Tim C.

THE COURT This is Tim C., the person you are speaking to.

COUNSEL Sorry.

And What Color Is an Orange?

(Delgado Smith, Texarkana, TX)

Q. When you were under the influence of meth and you needed to go to the bathroom, how did you know you needed to go?

A. I was potty-trained at two, probably.

Q. Did you ever step in front of a moving car when you were high?

A. I don't think so.

Q. Why not?

A. Hmm. Maybe because I would get run over.

Ordinary Lover's Quarrel

(Michael Chaney, Los Angeles)

Q. In San Francisco, did you not break down the bathroom door?

A. No, I did not.

Q. In San Francisco, you did not try to molest me?

A. Nothing out of the ordinary.

Hummmmmmm

(Delgado Smith, Texarkana, TX)

COUNSEL You were doing that—you were trying to protect the witness.

A. No, I was trying to protect myself.

COUNSEL Okay. Hummmmm.

THE COURT I've known you for some while.

COUNSEL Pardon me, Your Honor. I know what you're talking about. I was clearing my throat. I need a little water.

THE COURT You do not comment on the evidence. All right? You can only ask questions.

COUNSEL Yes. Your Honor.

THE COURT So refrain from commenting on the evidence.

COUNSEL I move that my "hummmmm" be stricken.

"On the question of redistributing wealth, Your Honor,
the witness will offer expert testimony."

{ 4 }

The Experts

I fear the day when technology overlaps with our humanity.
The world will consist of a generation of idiots.

ALBERT EINSTEIN

Anything is possible if you don't know what you are talking about.

ANON

It requires a very unusual mind to make an analysis of the obvious.

ALFRED NORTH WHITEHEAD

My psychiatrist told me I was crazy and I said I want a second opinion.
He said, okay, you're ugly too.

RODNEY DANGERFIELD

Expert Opinion

(J. Frank McCabe, San Francisco)

Q. Good morning, Doctor. What is your profession?

A. Forensic serologist

Q. What is a forensic serologist?

A. A forensic serologist is an individual who by virtue of his education and experience examines biological evidence.

Q. What is your current position?

A. Sitting.

Expert Testimony

(George Schraer, San Diego)

First, I want everybody to know that I did get an "A" in my bad writing class in medical school. There is nothing that I can do about it. I apologize for it in advance. Next, people that are very psychotic can often feed themselves. And I truly believe that many psychotic people drive Highway 24 on a consistent basis because I drive that road, and I see a lot of crazy drivers. But a person can do these two things and still be very psychotic.

Expert with Poor Recall

(Mark Shenfield, Guerneville)

Q. How many latent prints did you analyze?

A. I don't recall the specific number.

Q. So it's from one to fifty?

A. I believe it was less than two.

Q. So that would make it one?

A. I don't remember.

Q. You believe it's less than two and it's not zero.

A. That's correct.

Q. So that would make it one.

A. I don't recall.

Insightful Opinion

(Delgado Smith, Texarkana, TX)

[The expert] did not testify that defendant would or probably would commit violent acts in the future. Neither did he claim that sociopaths necessarily commit violent crimes. To the contrary, he testified that sociopaths could conform to legal requirements when controls and surveillance are high, an answer which suggests that they could conform in a prison setting. When asked, "Would a sociopath always by the mere fact that he is a sociopath engage in criminal behavior?" he replied, "Oh, no. I think some of the finest trial attorneys, car salesmen, business executives and politicians are among the most sociopathic members of our culture."

[People v. Daniels, 52 Cal.3d 815, 882 (1991)]

"Your Name"

(Katherine Houston, Ukiah)

Q. Can you tell us in general where the tattoo was?

A. Yes.

Q. Would you, please?

A. Not on the head of the penis. On the upper skin of the penis. I believe it's on the right side going long ways, two lines going long ways.

Q. You're talking about like the shaft of the penis, the long part?

A. That's correct.

Q. It's on the side as opposed to the top?

A. I didn't say it's on the side. I think it's on the upper, like, 45 degrees maybe off the top.

Q. Was it writing?

A. Yes. Two words.

Q. Or printing?

A. Two words.

Q. Was one word on one side and one on the other?

A. No.

Q. And what were the two words?

A. Your name. Y-o-u-r n-a-m-e. The penis was very soft, and I could not read "your name."

Q. Later on at the hospital, was there something different about the condition of the penis that allowed you to read that?

A. Nope, other than myself putting on latex gloves and stretching out the skin of the shaft, as you called it, and reading the words "your name."

Q. So even in a soft state, if you stretched out the skin, it was clearly readable to you?

A. To me. I was specifically looking for it, you know.

Q. Can you estimate right now how high the letters were—

A. Counsel, it would obviously change with the—

Q. When you saw it.

A. Maybe a quarter inch, three-eighths of an inch block letters.

Q. Printing?

A. Block letters.

Q. You were looking for this because why?

A. Because I had been told that the victim told [the detective] that your client had her name tattooed on his penis.

DSM-IV Explained

(Michael Thorman, Hayward)

Q. Does the term "passive-aggressive" have a technical meaning in the psychology area?

A. I'm sure it does.

Q. Were you using it in a technical way or sort of a non-technical way when you just described him as being passive-aggressive?

A. Well, let's just say it's an indirect expression of hostility. It's kind of gumming up the works as opposed to expressing yourself directly toward a person.

Q. Can you give me an example of what you mean by gumming up the works?

A. Let's say you have a job, you don't like your boss, you resent what he's asking you to do. You disagree with him. Instead of saying, you know, "I'm not going to do that; I don't think that's appropriate; I don't want to do it," you would sort of go along, take three times as long to do it, lose half the stuff, drop papers on the floor, just make it

pretty intolerable for the person to deal with you doing
something you didn't want to do.

COUNSEL Like being married.

A Dog Named Boz

(Jerry Shuford, Indio)

We'll call Officer Peters.

COUNSEL Thank you, Your Honor. Your Honor, I'm wondering in view of the space limitations here, perhaps
Officer Peters and Boz could come more over in the well
area and then once the jury has had the opportunity to
look at the dog, then Officer Peters will take Boz back
out to the police car, secure him, and come to the stand
to testify. Officer Peters, before you take Boz back out to
his perch in the patrol unit, can you command him to
bark for the jury.

[The dog barks on command]

COUNSEL Officer Peters, any way—he's facing such that he's
facing away from the jury. Is there any way you can position him so he's facing toward the jury and him do that.
Could he do that again, Your Honor?

[The dog barks on command]

THE COURT Do you need anything further?

DEFENSE COUNSEL Could we have him attack the District
Attorney?

THE COURT I don't think that would be necessary.

The Future Psychopath

(Dale M. Rubin, Los Angeles)

Q. What effect would an antisocial personality disorder have on an individual? What does that do?

A. A person with antisocial personality disorder if he is intellectually bright will become a politician. If he is not too bright, he would end up in jail.

Live and in Color

(David Carleton, Los Angeles)

COUNSEL Is your forensic analysis limited to cases where somebody is dead?

A. I don't understand the question.

COUNSEL Do you only do this in cases where somebody has died?

DA Objection, vague as to what, do what?

COUNSEL Your forensic autopsies.

Expert Witness (from Mars?)

(Hon. Martin Solomon, Brooklyn, NY)

Q. Over time, as he gets older, what is going to happen to his lumbar spine, his lower back?

A. The most likely course, the most common course, somebody that has these type of injuries, he is going to develop a severe arthritic process.

Q. Would you characterize that within a reasonable degree
   of medical certainty as a serious injury?
A. Well, I don't know, I can't answer that one. I don't really
   know that. When you say serious, everything is relative.
   Someone who has a cracked skull and lost three eyes—
THE COURT Three eyes? Where do you practice?
DOCTOR I mean, I can't answer that one.

Attorney Antisocialists

(Jim Thomson, Berkeley)

DA Would you agree with me that perhaps having some antisocial features can actually be of benefit to a criminal
   defense lawyer?
COUNSEL Objection. Insulting.
DA Excluding, of course, Learned Counsel from that
   question.
WITNESS No, I wouldn't agree with that. I don't think the
   way that our system is set up that using the law to its full-
   est extent represents being antisocial. I think the ability to
   be amoral and nonjudgmental is helpful. That is also
   helpful in being a good therapist or psychiatrist, just as I
   make no judgments as to whether it is right or wrong to
   have an affair or an abortion. But I certainly don't see
   antisocial personality traits aiding in the occupation of
   an attorney.

Memorable Advice

(J. Frank McCabe, San Francisco)

Q. Can you explain to the jurors what "state dependent memory" refers to?

A. Yes. Nothing to do with which of the fifty states you're living in. But certain memories may be more retrievable if you can replicate the state you were in at the time you made the initial memory. It is possibly a somewhat apocryphal bit of advice, but I think it may have some truth to it: If a law student is drinking a lot of beer while they're studying for the exam, they would do well to bring some beer into the examination, because they're much better able to recreate whatever it is they studied if they're in a similar state of intoxication.

THE COURT That's a novel thought.

WITNESS You see why I'm no longer teaching at the law school.

In Search for Expertise

(George Thompson, Barstow)

THE COURT I'd like to hear from somebody who knows assault rifles who would be able to testify as an expert. You have nobody?

DA Not at this time. I could—

THE COURT We have to do it in one continuous setting.

COUNSEL The People said they were ready.

THE COURT Is there any officer in the courtroom that has experience with assault rifles?

[No response]

COUNSEL Your Honor, I object to the Court requesting if there might be an expert in the courtroom to testify. The People said they were ready and know that their witness can't prove it's an assault weapon, I don't think we should run all over town to find somebody who can.

DA If there's someone present in the courtroom that has the expertise to testify—

THE COURT Step over to the individual who's approaching and have an inquiry.

Cocaine You Don't See

(Michael R. Berger, Oakland)

Q. So you add the requirement of a visible manipulable amount is a usable amount? Is that fair?

A. In my experience that is the case. Yes.

Q. Officer, in your opinion, is 1.32 grams of cocaine base a usable amount?

A. Yes.

Q. What is that opinion based upon?

A. My training and experience and all of the things that we have talked about, talked with dealers and users of cocaine.

Q. And would that opinion remain the same if that was 1.3 grams of invisible crack cocaine?

A. I never dealt with invisible crack cocaine, so I don't think I can answer that.

Profile of the Dull Pot Grower

(Donald Lipmanson, Navarro)

Q. You described the defendant as having the appearance of a marijuana cultivator?

A. Yes.

Q. How do you correlate scruffy hair and marijuana correlation?

A. I'd say the overall appearance of somebody that grows marijuana is normally somebody that's somewhat scruffy.

Q. There's a correlation between hiking boots and marijuana cultivation?

A. Marijuana is usually cultivated in rough terrain, and in that rough terrain you need, usually, the appropriate attire to get there. Hiking boots get you there.

Q. Soiled jeans. Are you saying there's a correlation between that and marijuana cultivation?

A. Somebody who does gardening, yes.

Q. The Kauai T-shirt, is that a correlation with the appearance of a marijuana cultivator?

A. I believe there was. It's like a tie-die type of bright color type thing.

Q. And his appearance was part of the basis of your pulling him over?

A. Yes, and the dull appearance.

Q. The dull appearance. If I could get you to say what are the components of the dull appearance? I'm not sure I understand that.

A. Well, as of right now, I would say you do not have a dull appearance. But given His Honor, maybe, a little bit.

Q. Does it mean that one is sort of not focusing very much on the surroundings?

A. Correct.

THE COURT If somebody is bored, can that make them look like they have a dull appearance?

A. I believe so.

What's in a Nickname?

(J. Frank McCabe, Burlingame)

COUNSEL It's almost universal that most people have a nickname?

GANG EXPERT I don't know. I don't have a nickname.

Q. Well, lots of people you know have nicknames, right?

A. I know people that have nicknames, yes.

Q. I mean, if I were to tell you that in college, I had friends named Psycho, Cue Ball, Uncle Gino, Weasel, and Hen, would that be an unusual type of thing in your experience or do most people have friends with those kind of nicknames?

A. I don't have any friends that have names like that. And I don't know about your college experience, so I couldn't comment on that.

THE COURT Psycho and Weasel?

COUNSEL Psycho and Weasel. Weasel is my accountant.

Multiple-Discipline Expert Witness

(Bonnie Miller, Montana)

A. No. I'm saying that if the true temperature outside is 90 degrees, and you say it's 89.999, you're wrong, but you're not very wrong. If you say it's 2 degrees, you're very wrong. In this context, the central limit theorem guarantees that the size, actual relative size of the error decreases to zero as the number of terms becomes large. So one wrong doesn't make a right. Two wrongs don't make a right, but they make a smaller relative error. Many wrongs, meaning many estimates, each one of which is likely to not be completely accurate, lead to a vanishingly small error for the average. That's the intuitive substance of several of the central limit theorems.

COUNSEL What is that word you said again? Something-ally? Vaginally? Is that what you said?

A. Vanishingly.

COUNSEL Oh, I'm sorry. I mean, I don't know math, but I mean—

A. All I'm telling you is, when your vaginally and your vanishingly become confused in your mind, you have deeper issues than the ones we're dealing with here.

Keister In

(Mike Crain, Los Angeles)

Q. In that incident, he comes over to you. You have to ask him three times if he wants a knife?

A. Yes.

Q. Correct?

A. Yes.

Q. You're keistering a knife at this time?

A. I'm pulling a piece out.

Q. You're keistering. If you're pulling it out, you're keistering it?

A. No, keister's going in.

Q. Is there a word for coming out?

A. Pull it out.

Q. All right.

A. Ouch.

Q. I can only imagine.

A. No, you couldn't.

Q. I bet I can't. And you're, if I can picture this, you're reaching and pulling a knife out in front of everybody there on the rec yard?

A. I'll attribute it to this. I had an experience where I reached, trying to pull a piece out like at knife. When you go back to your cell, you know, you take the piece out for the night. Okay. I reached in one time and tried to find that knife and it wasn't there. That will scare the shit out of you.

Q. Literally?

Size Matters

(Sara Azari, Los Angeles)

Q. She had an erect penis stuck inside her mouth. Would you expect her to describe it being like a pencil in her mouth?

A. Well, it depends on the man.

Fecal Reconstruction Expert

(Don Levine, San Diego)

Q. In the defense exhibit, there appears to be some fecal matter in there.

A. Correct.

Q. And it does appear to be toward the center of the diaper, correct?

A. The center toward the rear, yes.

Q. Does it appear to be sort of a rather large portion or a large piece of fecal matter?

COUNSEL Objection, vague as to the word "large."

THE COURT Sustained.

Q. How would you describe the size of that piece of fecal matter in the diaper? Does it expand from the width of one side of the diaper to the other?

A. Pretty much. It is probably a half to two-thirds of it.

Q. Based on this photograph, does it appear to be a solid piece that's being depicted in the photograph?

COUNSEL Objection, no foundation.

THE COURT Sustained.

Q. I'm pointing to a portion right in the very middle of the diaper. There appears to be a large fecal matter.

A. Yes.

Q. Does that appear to be one continuous piece of fecal matter or it is numerous pieces?

COUNSEL Objection. Foundation. The photograph speaks for itself. This was frozen and the diaper bundled back together. I can voir-dire the witness to show that the fecal matter can be reconstituted, so to speak; in other words, stuck back together to form one piece where it was two.

THE COURT Overruled. If you know, Doctor, you can answer the question.

A. I can't answer. I can't tell if it was one or multiple pieces because of what Counsel stated.

Q. Does it appear that that in there is what I would call a symptom of diarrhea?

A. No.

New Potty Disorder Diagnosed

(Melissa Nappan, Sacramento)

In addition, he acknowledged having a disability of Post Traumatic Stress Disorder, extreme depression and Attention Defecate Disorder.

I Want a Witness Too

(Ken Quigley, San Francisco)

THE COURT Lay opinion is admissible on the question of identification of the person in the photo. That does not invade the province of the jury. And I should say that the principle extends to the defense. So that if there were a defense witness who would be willing to take the stand and say that the person in the photograph is not the defendant, that would equally qualify.

DEFENSE COUNSEL I'll see if I can go hire one.

Dog Bites Non-Whites Only

(Donald Cook, Los Angeles)

A. I have studied most extensively the County Sheriff's and the LAPD's use of canines, and I probably have a lot of knowledge about those two programs, certainly more so about those programs than any other law enforcement canine program. They are both frightening in what they permit. It's hard to imagine how a policy could be worse, but I suppose it could be. Certainly the Sheriff's policy is worse than the LAPD. There are some aspects of LAPD policy that are commendable as compared to other canine programs.

Q. Such as?

A. Well, LAPD will make it explicit you do not use dogs in crowd control situations, and there are a lot of smaller departments that do permit the use of dogs in crowd control situations. That's an example.

Q. Anything else?

A. Well, I think, in just reviewing the Search Data Reports, there appears to be a conscious effort on the part of LAPD not to employ dogs to bite Caucasians who are suspected of minor offenses.

Q. You find that commendable?

A. Well, certainly, as compared to a municipality that uses its dogs to bite anybody who is suspected of a minor offense. At least the LAPD will make an exception if you're white. I mean, that's a benefit to those who are white. I realize there are some equal protection problems there, but let's face it, some people get off the hook of getting bit. That's better than having them all bit, don't you think?

The Gang Expert Gives It Up

(Paul Potter, Pasadena)

Q. Your opinion is that all violence which is engaged in by people who you identify as gang members is committed for the benefit of the gang?

A. Yes.

Q. That is regardless of the individual circumstances of any particular incident?

A. That is correct.

Q. So if a gang member comes home and gets in a fight with his wife and slaps her in the side of the head, that is done for the benefit of the gang, correct?

A. That is incorrect, sir.

Q. Is that violence?

A. It is domestic violence.

Q. That doesn't count?

A. Whatever happens in their home, it doesn't relate to a gang-related crime. It will not benefit their gang.

Q. So a gang member comes down and sees his brother-in-law in the parking lot at Costco, and he says, "I heard you hit my sister. You can't do that," and picks up a tire iron and he gives his brother-in-law a nice strong knock in the public parking lot at Costco. Is that an act which occurs for the benefit of the gang?

A. Again, it is a family dispute–related crime.

Q. A gang member takes too many drugs and starts hallucinating and believes that the lady sitting on the bus bench is a wild rhinoceros, and he throws her to the ground. Is that an act which is committed for the benefit of the gang?

A. I guess not.

Q. So I can think of more examples. Would it be fair to say, then, that not all violence committed by gang members is necessarily committed for the benefit of the gang?

A. That's correct.

Q. So would you like to withdraw your previous answer that all violence committed by gang members is committed for the benefit of the gang?

A. All violence committed by gang members upon rival gang members is committed for benefit of the gang.

Q. Unless they are hallucinating and think they are assaulting rhinoceri?

A. Yes. That's correct.

Autopsy Status (Redux)

(J. Frank McCabe, San Francisco)

Q. And did the doctor prepare a report in the performance of the autopsy?

A. Yes, sir, he did.

Q. Did you review that report when interviewing the doctor about the details of the autopsy in this case?

A. Yes, sir. I did.

Q. What did the doctor tell you in your interview was the condition of the body when he performed the autopsy?

A. He described it as dead.

"Swiftest Justice on the Sixth Appellate Court."

{ 5 }

The Judges

This Court has never held that the Constitution forbids the execution of a convicted defendant who has had a full and fair trial but is later able to convince a habeas court that he is "actually" innocent.

IN RE DAVIS, 130 S.CT. 1, 3 (2009) (SCALIA DISSENTING)

I was married by a judge. I should have asked for a jury.

GROUCHO MARX

Judges have the "abysmal gravity not found in any other profession save that of the undertaker."

ANON

Lord Westbury, it is said, rebuffed a barrister's reliance upon an earlier opinion of his by stating, "I can only say that I am amazed that a man of my intelligence should have been guilty of giving such an opinion."

IN KING V. CENTRAL BANK, 18 CAL.3D 840, 850 (1977) (MOSK CONCURRING)

Court Order on News of Settlement

(Ephraim Margolin, San Francisco)

Such news of an amicable settlement having made this court happier than a tick on a fat dog because it is otherwise busier than a one-legged cat in a sand box and, quite frankly, would have rather jumped naked off of a twelve foot step ladder into a five gallon bucket of porcupines than have presided over a two week trial of the herein dispute, a trial which, no doubt, would have made the jury more confused than a hungry baby in a topless bar and made the parties and their attorneys madder than mosquitoes in a mannequin factory. The clerk shall engage the services of a structural engineer to ascertain if the return of this file to the Clerk's office will exceed the maximum structural load of the floor of said office.

Judge Wins Reelection While Pleading Insanity

[*Huffington Post*, Chicago, Nov. 12, 2012]

A Cook County Circuit Court judge was handily reelected Tuesday a matter of hours before she was due to appear in court for allegedly assaulting a deputy sheriff this spring, an attack her attorney previously blamed on the fact that the judge was "legally insane" at the time.

[Judge] Brim's attorney James Montgomery said Wednesday that his client has bipolar disorder, a condition she has controlled with medication, but that at the time of the attack she was "legally insane," the *Tribune* reports.

In twenty-two years, a sitting circuit court judge in Cook County has lost reelection only once.

Naming Names

(George Schraer, San Diego)

THE COURT if you have no objection doing the Martinez case, I could release him.

COUNSEL Jimenez, Your Honor. The witness is Jimenez, not Martinez.

THE COURT Well, I am going to call him Martinez.

COUNSEL Every time we say Martinez we mean Jimenez?

THE COURT Martinez is easier to say than Jimenez.

Sloppy Lies Are Best

(Howard Price, Beverly Hills)

THE COURT I indicated before, and the deputy is here, I think that's probably one of the sloppiest reports I have ever seen and I don't want to use the word "appalled," but I am really upset that you would testify at one point during the preliminary hearing so different from the testimony in the subsequent suppression hearings.

In any event, it's my view that cocaine dealing is not a rational process in and of itself. A number of years ago there wouldn't be anyone who could convince me that in the city of Inglewood where this occurred, that certain areas of Inglewood—and I am not singling out Inglewood by a long shot—just of any cities—and I have had it happen to myself, you drive down the street, the people come out and bang on your window and try to sell you cocaine.

A number of years ago we would have told each other that would not occur, people would not do anything such as that, that it would be so silly that people would expose themselves in that manner, and they do it an incredible number of times.

In any event, as I indicated before, I think the testimony of the officer was very negligently given. I am very distressed by it. I think it shows, in my opinion, a somewhat sloppy preparation on the part of the deputy. I'm telling you that right now.

I don't want to use the word "appalled," but I'm close to appalled by the sloppiness that occurred in this, but the net result of listening to this—if I thought he was lying, he looks to me like a relatively intelligent deputy. If he had lied, he would have come up with a much more rational lie than he came up with. I believe his testimony given here and the motion is denied. Thank you.

Sins of the Father

(Paul Bell, San Diego)

THE COURT And then there was one other juror name I was going to ask Counsel if they would mind if we did not have to call in here. That's Coach Doe. I only say that because this Court has had both private and public disagreements with Coach Doe over my son when he played basketball a few years ago. We get along all right, but I imagine he would feel uncomfortable as I would because both in the press and privately we've had our disagreements. And I'm sure we have got over those, but—

COUNSEL I'd stipulate, Your Honor.

THE COURT Okay. I think it would be easier on everybody probably. So we'll go ahead and tell Coach Doe he can go down to the jury assembly room. Yes. Try not to get him out on a year-long case.

Q & A

(Robert M. Leen, Seattle, WA)

Q. This letter, purportedly from the same man, must have been reviewing something to make those two corrections. In less than ten days he writes another letter, and it's a considerably different style, referring to the same things, isn't it?

A. Is that a rhetorical question?

Q. Yes, and you've answered it correctly.

No One Gets Out Alive

(Gary Sowards, San Francisco)

THE COURT After we select a jury and the alternates, then the District Attorney will probably make an opening statement to the jury, telling the jury what he expects the evidence is going to show in this case. When he finishes his opening statement, then I will call upon the defendant's attorney, and he has an option. He can make an opening statement to you, telling you what he believes the evidence is going to show on behalf of his client, or he can reserve his opening statement until after the People put—

[A voice from the audience] Excuse me, Your Honor, I am going to leave.

THE COURT Find out about him, Mr. Bailiff.

[The voice] Jesus Christ.

Expertise Stuff

(Marvin Marks, Stockton)

THE COURT What's the point of it?

DA Countersurveillance driving.

THE COURT Countersurveillance driving.

DA The agent has previously qualified in federal court, and a published opinion said that it was proper expert testimony.

COUNSEL YOU mean you're going to ask him if this car turned a lot of corners trying to ditch him?

THE COURT I'll let you bring out all the driving—I've read every spy book published since 1945—

DA Maybe now this is a subject we don't really need expert—

THE COURT You don't really need to get into that. I read a book last week about a front tail where you tail the guy by driving in front of him. And then I was thinking about *The Godfather* when he was going to the restaurant and they made the U-turn on the Brooklyn Bridge. But I don't think you need to get into that expertise sort of stuff.

Vocal Deadly Weapons and Marital Arts

(Jack L. Schwartz, Los Angeles)

THE COURT Counsel and I have had a meeting on jury instructions in chambers. And this Court has no authority for the proposition that the mouth as a general proposition is a deadly weapon, and no evidence to show that the defendant has been trained in the marital arts or some other form of arts so that he knows how to use his mouth as a deadly weapon.

Musings on a Motion to Withdraw

(Janice Hogan, San Diego)

THE COURT And there is a policy matter that we have to consider here. You know, the Ninth Circuit Court of Appeals judges can sit up there in their ivory towers until hell freezes over and they don't know the first thing of what goes on in a trial court because nine out of ten of them never sat in a trial court. One of which is my brother. But all I have to do, for example, is to allow this man, under some sort of guise that I really didn't believe, but to so-called overly protect the record to withdraw his guilty plea. But then every time I would tell somebody that they cannot withdraw their guilty plea when they come in here, that wouldn't mean a thing because once he goes back to the jail it's going to spread like wildfire and I would venture to guess, except in extremely unusual circumstances, I would be constantly bombarded with with-drawing guilty pleas. I don't believe in that.

Now, this is not the case like the last one I set aside which was, I don't know, perhaps a year ago or so where the facts of that one were very simple—the guy appeared in Magistrate's Court, his attorney was from L.A., which is in itself suspect, and the L.A. lawyer says, well, he says, you go ahead and plead guilty right today and you'll be out day after tomorrow. Well, what he didn't tell the defendant was that in order to get out, the defendant had to cooperate.

Don't Ask

(Kim Malcheski, San Francisco)

THE COURT How am I doing? You know, it's funny you ask. I work out every other day. I am getting a little too old for this stuff. I think I did something with the rotator cuff yesterday. I have these two teenage brats that don't really understand me. We are going to get to that later. These two teenagers are really brats, I don't know what to do. It was raining all weekend, I spent most of the time at home. I am not doing too well. I had a dog that had to have an operation on its knees. I didn't even know dogs had knees but thanks for asking.

Nothing in Pocket

(John Henry Hingson III, Oregon City, OR)

THE COURT If I'm the trial judge—and Judge F. is a wonder-
ful human being and I'd rather have him be an uncle to
my children than anybody I can think of, but, quite
frankly, if I get to the position that Judge F. is in, I'm going
to look at Counsel and say, "Counsel, do you want a mistrial or do you want to ask your next question?" and put
the turd in his pocket, and where I've got a clear record
that he's made his choice. Whatever it is, he's made it, and
we go from there. And that didn't happen here.

Pay No Attention to the Man in Chains

(Mark Arnold, Bakersfield)

The Court admonished the jury panel that it is the policy of the
Court and the sheriff's department that all in custody defendants
are to be handcuffed and shackled when being transported along
public hallways. The jury is to disregard that fact when deliberating
upon a verdict.

Naming Names

(George Schraer, San Diego)

Q. Mr. S., are you Cambodian?
A. Yes, sir.

Q. This man over to the left, are you related to him in any
   way?

A. That's my younger brother.

Q. How much younger is he than you?

A. He's next to me, about one year, two years.

Q. You one or two years older than him?

A. Yes.

Q. And could you tell us why your name is spelled different
   than his?

A. Actually, we have the same last name but somehow when
   we came to the United States, something wrong with the
   immigration. The whole family got the same last name,
   but somehow they fuck up, I don't know.

THE COURT That's a good word when you discuss government, actually.

Shrunken Head

(Anonymous Bosch, Paris, ID)

COUNSEL Good morning, Doctor [a pyschiatrist].

A. Good morning.

COUNSEL I understand you and the Judge have developed
   quite a long relationship. You have testified in this courtroom before and you know each other; is that right?

A. Yes.

Q. Did you want to take some time to visit with your friend?

THE COURT No, go ahead it's all right. I don't need any therapy today.

COUNSEL That is not a universal conclusion, Your Honor.

Case Closed

(Charles Feer, Bakersfield)

COURT: This is going to be a disaster because I start the calendar in division G at one-thirty. We got to take prisoners out of the building. You don't need any more witnesses. If you call any more witnesses, I am probably going to have someone fire a round or two at you. We don't need any more. He has identified this guy.

Shooting Gallery

(George Schraer, San Diego)

THE COURT I see that the detective is here. Detective, if you'll come forward, please.
DA Your Honor, at this point I have no further witnesses.
THE COURT You have no further witnesses?
DA The People have laid the foundation and met the foundational requirements.
THE COURT Detective, do you want to shoot him? It's all right with me.

Not a Chance

(George Schraer, San Diego)

COUNSEL Judge, would this be a good time for a break?
THE COURT We'll take a short recess.
[whereupon, a recess was taken]

THE COURT You may continue.

COUNSEL Thank you. The court reporter indicated that I was going a little too fast before and asked me to reread my argument, so I'll start from the beginning, if I may.

THE COURT I overrule my court reporter.

Follow the Leader

(Stephen Greenberg, Nevada City)

Q. What I'm asking is, during that interview did we tell him that witnesses had told us that?

A. No.

Q. You don't recall one of us telling him witnesses said they had seen that?

COUNSEL Objection.

THE COURT That's an improper question. He said you're saying do you remember that one of us did tell? That's leading because you're suggesting that one of you did tell. And that, jury, is an example of a leading and suggestive question. It suggests the answer to be given. And my taking the time to explain this to you will give the officer on the stand an opportunity to review his report and get the answer right.

Frozen Out

(Delgado Smith, Texarkana, TX)

A. I had telephoned her and I believe I had said something such as . . .

COUNSEL Excuse me. Hearsay.

THE COURT Overruled.

WITNESS I believe I telephoned her on that date and I told her that I had talked to . . .

COUNSEL My objection is now double hearsay.

THE COURT Overruled doubly.

Q. Okay. Is that phone that is seen in this photograph, is that phone—are you cold?

A. Very.

Q. I'm glad that it isn't me that's making you shake.

THE COURT I see jurors putting coats jackets on. Sometimes we hang meat in here after a four-day weekend.

Judicial Rant over the Returning Illegals

(Delgado Smith, Texarkana, TX)

I mean, this is like fighting the Vietnam War. You're fighting the war, but you are not trying to win. That is not what I am doing. I am trying to win the war. I'm not sitting here just blowing smoke, you know. That's what it sounds like is happening in this case. I don't care what their reasons are for coming back. I suppose we can send him back across the border and chain him to a tree on the other side of the border. That would certainly prevent him from coming back. This is the kind of thing that the Congress and the Justice Department and the Attorney General ought to know about because you can put these people all across the border and do all this Mickey Mouse stuff and you can build fences, you can waste a lot of the government's money, but unless you have somebody standing right there with a gun in their hand—and I don't care whether they call it protecting the border or whatever they call it—and a gun that will shoot, you're going to get this same situation. Sentence a guy and he comes back here, he's through. He gets the maximum. So don't bother bargaining, we'll take him to trial. I will try every one of them because this is like shoveling sand against the tide. No breaks; no second time. Once I sentence them, they are gone. They are going to stay gone. I'm going to tell everybody in this courtroom personally, I really don't care what the guidelines say anymore. I don't care what your numbers are. You come back here again and I'm going to sentence you to five years in prison. You take it up on appeal and I will get reversed. By the time I get reversed, you will have done most of the five years. So don't tempt me.

Judicial Notice

(David Stanley, Sacramento)

Q. At the point in time your daughter came, would you say you were under the influence?

A. From one can of beer?

Q. It's Old English 800.

A. Man, I've been drinking Old English 800 for I don't know how long, and it ain't did nothing yet.

Q. It's your testimony that you were in pretty good condition—

A. I was sober as a judge.

COUNSEL I think we can take that as being pretty sober, is that correct, Your Honor?

Animal, Vegetable, or Mineral?

(Jack Campbell, Vista)

THE COURT I have a question about count one. If you read the statute, it makes reference to "animals" and I believe that—I haven't looked at Mr. Webster this morning, but I don't believe a parrot is an animal. Do you have any authority that would classify a parrot as an animal?

DA If I could just check the annotations on that, Your Honor.

THE COURT With respect to count one, the Court will discharge the defendant. The Court makes a legal conclusion as opposed to finding of fact that a parrot is not an animal.

Juror Sacrifice

(Bruce Cormicle, Riverside)

THE COURT Ladies and gentlemen, normally at this time we would actually take probably eighteen of you and have you killed at random and seated in the jury box. We are going to have a little different procedure here because of the time qualification aspect of this case. We are going to do that first.

A Car Is Not a Home

(Jim Thompson, Berkeley)

With respect to automobiles generally, it may safely be said that Hoosiers regard their automobiles as private and cannot readily abide their uninvited intrusion. As footnote 3 reads: "Americans in general love their cars. It is, however, particularly important, in the state which hosts the Indy 500 automobile race, to recognize that cars are sources of pride, status, and identity that transcended their objective attributes. We are extremely hesitant to countenance their casual violation, even by law enforcement officers who are attempting to solve serious crimes."

[*Brown State*, 653 N.E.2d 72, 80 (Ind. 1995)]

Nothing Sensational

(Charles M. Bonneau, Sacramento)

While the offenses were serious, that factor is not dispositive . . . and the print and television media articles were factual, not inflammatory. There was no sensationalism beyond reporting the fact that the heads and hands had been removed from the bodies.

[*People v. Hayes*, 21 Cal.4th 1211, 1251 (1999)]

Where the Sun Don't Shine

(Ed Bronson, Chico)

COUNSEL Does the Court have a preference as to where these videotapes should be?
THE COURT Yes, but I don't think it's physically possible.

Cruel & Unusual

(Delgado Smith, Texarkana, TX)

COUNSEL May I have just one moment, Your Honor, before we begin?

THE COURT Yes. You want a second now?

COUNSEL I just want to go to the bathroom.

THE COURT Do you want me to call a press conference?

COUNSEL I suppose we could brief the matter. But there is the Eighth Amendment, cruel and unusual punishment. I defer to Your Honor's discretion.

THE COURT Then let's make it cruel and unusual.

Damned with Faint Praise

(Tara Mulay, San Francisco)

THE COURT I don't like what your attorney has done in the use of his peremptory challenges. I think what he did was illegal, and quite frankly, I think it was immoral. But that does not mean he is not a capable attorney.

Felony Dumb

(Tamara Holland, Emeryville)

THE COURT I'm not inclined to send him to the twenty-five years to life.

COUNSEL Thank you very much.

THE COURT Through no fault of his own. If stupidity were his crime, there wouldn't be enough years to give him.

Butter Up the Judge

(Stephen P. McCue, Albuquerque, NM)

THE COURT I hate to have you call someone younger than I am old; see, that's why I wanted to point that out.

COUNSEL I was going to say that this is a young man in the prime of his life, Your Honor.

THE COURT That's fair. I like that.

DEFENDANT I do, too.

Take These Chains

(Mark Reichel, Sacramento)

THE COURT And I am ordering that the defendant not to be chained. I've determined that there is no way that the Court can prevent exposure to assure that the jurors will not be able to see the chains, and there's no way that the Court can have a trial if he is chained. So I'm ordering that he not be chained. The marshals can get enough people in here. It was the marshal that called it to the attention of the clerk that the jurors saw the chains. Now, if there's a problem, they can just shoot him. That's the way to get the security. If he creates a problem, shoot him. Don't smile, Mr. Defendant, because if you create a problem, you're a dead man.

Trick Order

(Carol Strickman, Oakland)

DEFENDANT I . . .

THE COURT Whoa, whoa. Wait, wait. Just a minute. I don't want to know what you think, hear, or care about any witness that testifies in this case. If you are going to testify under oath, which it is your right to do, you will discuss that with your lawyer and you will do it appropriately. I don't want to hear anything else you say. I don't want to know verbally or nonverbally.

DEFENDANT I'm done.

THE COURT You are done. Let me suggest this to you, sir. You will conduct yourself in the manner that the Court believes to be appropriate if you want to stay in your preliminary hearing. And I'm ordering that you not say another word out loud again. Do you understand?

DEFENDANT *[nods his head up and down]*

THE COURT You have to answer out loud.

Yogi Speaks: Half One Way,
a Quarter the Other?

(Carl Hancock, San Diego)

THE COURT *[to the jury]* With regard to count two, that was 6–6 in the last one. In what direction?

FOREPERSON It was kind of split down the middle to acquit and to convict.

Federal Court Order

(J. Frank McCabe, San Francisco)

This matter comes before the Court on Plaintiff's Motion to designate location of a deposition. Upon consideration of the Motion—the latest in a series of Gordian knots that the parties have been unable to untangle without enlisting the assistance of the federal courts—it is ORDERED that said Motion is DENIED. Instead, the Court will fashion a new form of alternative dispute resolution, to wit: at 4:00 p.m. on Friday, June 30, Counsel shall convene at a neutral site agreeable to both parties. If Counsel cannot agree on a neutral site, they shall meet on the front steps of the Sam M. Gibbons U.S. Courthouse, 801 North Florida Ave., Tampa, Florida 33602. Each lawyer shall be entitled to be accompanied by one paralegal who shall act as an attendant and witness. At that time and location, Counsel shall engage in one game of "rock, paper, scissors." The winner of this engagement shall be entitled to select the location for the deposition to be held somewhere in Hillsborough County during the period July 11–12. If either party disputes the outcome of this engagement, an appeal may be filed and a hearing will be held at 8:30 a.m. on Friday, July 7, before the undersigned.

Up in Smoke

(Richard Parsons, Peoria, Illinois)

Divorce rates are disturbingly high. Sometimes, marital splits get nasty when an ex-spouse decides to dish out a little dose of discomfort to his or her former partner. And as far as dishing out discomfort is concerned, the havoc visited on Chicago lawyer Richard Connors by his ex-wife would win a gold medal for creativity. With substantial assistance from his ex, Connors stands convicted in federal court of (among other things) violating a law we seldom encounter, the Trading with the Enemy Act [for illegally importing cigars from Cuba]."

[*United States v. Connors*, 441 F.3d 527, 529 (7th Cir. 2006)]

What If We Sang "Hail to the Chief" to "It's Hard out Here for a Pimp"?

Tomic v. Catholic Diocese of Peoria, 442 F.3d 1036, 1040 (7th Cir. 2006)

At argument, Tomic's lawyer astonished us by arguing that music has in itself no religious significance—its only religious significance is in its words. The implication is that it is a matter of indifference to the Church and its flock whether the words of the Gospel are set to Handel's Messiah or to "Three Blind Mice."

Judicial Poetry for Juvenile Lawyers

(Leslie Caldwell, Fairfield)

Stallions can drink water from a creek without a ripple;
The lawyers in this case must have a bottle with a nipple.
Babies learn to work by scooting and falling;
These lawyers practice law by simply mauling
Each other and the judge, but this must end soon
(Maybe facing off with six-shooters at noon?)
Surely lawyers who practice in federal court can take
A deposition without a judge's order, for goodness sake.

First, the arguments about taking the deposition at all,
And now this—establishing their experience to be small.
So, let me tell you both and be abundantly clear:
If you can't work this without me, I will be near.
There will be a hearing with pablum to eat
And a very cool cell where you can meet AND WORK OUT
YOUR INFANTILE PROBLEM WITH THE DEPOSITION.

[Order in *Keystone Media International, LLC v. Hancock*, No. 06-CA-594
SS, U.S. Dist. Ct.,West District Texas, 27 April 2007]

Suppose You Held a Jar?

[*Cecaj v. Gonzales*, 440 F.3d 897, 899 (7th Cir. 2006)]

The immigration judge's analysis of the evidence was radically defi-
cient. He failed to consider the evidence as a whole, as he was
required to do by the elementary principles of administrative law.
Instead he broke it into fragments. Suppose you saw someone holding a jar, and you said, "That's a nice jar," and he smashed it to
smithereens and said, "No, it's not a jar." That is what the immigration judge did.

Court Voir Dire

(Delgado Smith, Texarkana, TX)

THE COURT I'm not going to stand up in order to try to look
more intimidating, but I just want to get this post out of
my way. . . . In case you get really mad at me, understand
that the guy standing next to me carries. Okay. Why do

you feel that you could not commit to the time frame [to be a juror]?

JUROR Well, right now I'm going through a divorce.

THE COURT Well, then you got time on your hands. If you have your phone on.

JUROR I turned it off.

THE COURT We'll shoot your phone right now. We'll take care of it. Come on up here and we'll take care of it. It's alive. I am truly sorry for your loss. Thank you.

Approach to Legislative History

(Felix Frankfurter)

But this is a case for applying the canon of construction of the wag who said, when the legislative history is doubtful, go to the statute.

[*Greenwood v. United States*, 350 U.S. 366, 374 (1956)]

Back to the Future

(Terri Towery, Los Angeles)

COUNSEL Your Honor, what time would you like to call a time-out this afternoon?

THE COURT In ten minutes. Are you suggesting this is a better time?

COUNSEL No, I just need to know when I should sit down and stop asking any more questions.

THE COURT Fifteen minutes ago.

The Indisputable Rationale of Decision

(Gordon Brownell, San Mateo)

COUNSEL We would like to continue.

THE COURT I know he wants to put sentencing over completely.

COUNSEL Your Honor, he has personal problems he has to take care of.

THE COURT I do not intend to grant the continuance based on the grounds stated. I do not find that's good cause.

DEFENDANT I'm denied?

THE COURT Yes.

DEFENDANT On what grounds?

THE COURT On the grounds that I am the Judge.

Stayin' Alive

(Anonymous Bosch, Todo El Mundo)

THE COURT [to Counsel] I've inherited the Aryan Brotherhood trial. That's a six-month trial. It starts with the first thirteen defendants. One defendant just hung himself, so we have twelve. Another three are in the process of pleading, if we can keep them alive.

A Judge's Tirade

(Earl Bute, Paradise)

THE COURT Do you accept or reject the conditions of probation?

DEFENDANT I accept them.

THE COURT All right. Then, the Court wishes you success on your probation.

The Court now turns to the matter of your own recognizance. I have some things to say on the record. The Court orders the court reporter to transcribe all of the proceedings in this case; to file the transcript in this case; to deliver a certified copy thereof to the District Attorney of this County.

The DA does not appear today. He did not appear at the last proceeding. He has appeared one time in this case; nevertheless, when he did appear, he did not oppose a continuance. I stepped forward in faith in this case concerning the defendant's recognizance. I regret neither the wisdom nor the courage of that decision. I want this record to show that I'm fully aware of the blindsided attack upon me personally in the ongoing weekly DA publicity parade in the local press. The statements are contemptuous of this Court. I have never in my years on the bench held an attorney in contempt. I do not do so now. It's evidently open season on judges. I suppose the DA thinks that he's exercising free speech. I accept that at face value, and I exercise a little of my own right now on this record.

The DA doesn't know whereof he speaks; that's a legal phrase for saying he doesn't know what the hell he's talking about. He made six appearances in this case; one, for a continuance, which he did not oppose. He wasn't here at the last proceeding. He doesn't know the problems faced by the Court, and yet he calls an *ex parte* unilateral press conference to attack me personally.

I want to say that I'm going on sixty-one years old, and I have sat up here a number of years with the life that God has given me to decide these cases. I have made thousands of decisions. They haven't all been right, but every one of them has been a considered decision; a reflective decision. And I spell out for the DA, on this record, the consideration that I had and made and thought about in releasing the defendant on his recognizance.

I considered those things when I decided to release the defendant on his recognizance. He has made good his pledge. I don't regret that decision at all. I feel it was proper. I order this article which the DA had on the front page of the newspaper filed in this file for future reference, and I say to him as follows:

I do not know your motivations to yield such unbridled hatred and a personal attack on me, but I tell you the following:

One. I decline to do your bidding. Put me at the top of your list of those who decline to do your bidding. I sit up here and make independent judgment.

Two. The duly elected judges in this County and the men and women of the jury make the decisions in this Court, and not the District Attorney.

Three. I will continue to reject your ultraliberal plea bargains whenever they come before me.

Four. You may intimidate others with your angry and bullying tactics, but you don't intimidate this Court. No matter how many times you throw down your books, and stalk out of the courtroom, and slam the door, or call a unilateral press conference for the DA ego trip, that won't affect this Court's decision.

I don't know your reason for attack upon the Court and judges. Perhaps it is your lack of jury trial success. You have had two cases in this department. You have lost them both. One was a hung jury with a subsequent dismissal. One was a not guilty verdict. In each instance you stomped out the door like an angry petulant child. I give you fair warning I will not tolerate that conduct further. Nor am I alone.

I note in the newspaper again after the one verdict came in where the jury again did not agree with your theory of the case, but you chose to attack the trial judge and blame that verdict on an instruction that he gave, rather than yourself. I suggest it is time for you to look within; toward your own ineptitude, rather than blame judges and juries. Otherwise, life is going to become intolerable for you, and sooner or later you are bound to self-destruct.

Takes One to Know One

(Al & Jackie Menaster, Los Angeles)

BAILIFF Juror *[who is Asian]* says she does not speak English.
THE COURT *[who is Asian]* That'll be denied.
COUNSEL I request to voir-dire her.
THE COURT That'll be denied. The Asians pull that all the time.

Bad Judge Jokes

[*Ryan v. Comm'n on Judicial Performance*, 45 Cal.3d 518, 544(1988)]

No. 1: The judge admits telling the following joke while two female attorneys, among others, were present in his chambers: "It's during the period of creation and God has just gone ahead and . . . made the earth and the stars and the wind and some of the animals. He's still creating things. Adam and Eve have been created. They discover each other and they discover the physical portions of each other and they lay down and they make love. When they finish, Eve leaves for a little while and then returns. When she returns . . . Adam says, where have you been? She says, I went to the stream to wash off. And Adam says, gee, I wonder if that's going to give a scent to the fish?" The two female attorneys were offended by the joke.

No. 2: [T]wo female attorneys, among others, appeared before the judge in his chambers to conduct a preliminary hearing. Judge Ryan asked the two female attorneys if they knew the difference "between a Caesar salad and a blow job." When the attorneys responded that they did not know the difference, the judge said, "Great, let's have lunch." The attorneys were offended.

Expletives Included

(Charles Bonneau, Sacramento)

DA The witness is very short.

COUNSEL She may be short, but she's not necessary.

DA Your Honor, it's my case, and I'm trying to prove a complete case. It is a homicide case, Judge. It's not something where we can stipulate everything.

THE COURT That only means you're supposed to introduce relevant evidence.

DA That's what I'm trying to do.

THE COURT Half the stuff today, I don't care if she sent back $500,000 to Ohio. What the Christ does that have to do with July 31st?

DA I didn't bring it up.

THE COURT I know, and you bit.

DA I didn't know what it was about.

THE COURT Just like all these gullible DA's bite. If the defense attorney brings up something, they spend a half hour on it when it doesn't mean a goddamn thing.

COUNSEL Careful, Judge, you might shoot somebody later.

Legal Reasoning

(Richard Krech, Oakland)

Order: The People orally motioned to dismiss for insufficiency of the evidence a violation of probation. Defendant is not on probation in that case. The Court granted the motion and dismissed the violation of probation for insufficient evidence.

Greek to Me

(Stephen Bedrick, Oakland)

COUNSEL Since the prosecutor is sitting at a distance of approximately four feet from that position, I ask the Court to judicially notice the Pythagorean theorem which would leave him sitting approximately 20 feet from the witness.

THE COURT No way for the Court to take judicial notice of that which is a physical and mental impossibility which is why I was a liberal arts major.

Right to Public Trial? Ha! Ha!

(Hon. Maria Stratton, Los Angeles)

"In all criminal prosecutions the accused shall enjoy the right to a speedy and public jury trial."

[Sixth Amendment, U.S. Constitution]

COUNSEL First of all, Your Honor, there is no evidence that there's a security issue here. I think the appropriate remedy [is getting more security people] rather than excluding my client's family from these public proceedings.

THE COURT I understand you, but I suggest to you that the day you have as much experience with this issue as this marshal, I will listen to you. Until then, I won't.

COUNSEL Your Honor, I think that will be fundamentally unfair.

THE COURT Too bad.

COUNSEL If the Court wants black letter law, the Constitution provides for . . .

THE COURT *[Laughter]*

The Grinch & the Judge

(Hon. Maria Stratton, Los Angeles)

PROSECUTOR Your Honor, I object to the defense's cultural expert. The fact that his client may have been poor and desperately looking for work as a day laborer to put food on the table is irrelevant to these proceedings.

THE COURT Counsel, I grew up in East Los Angeles. I and my friends know and understand what it means to be poor and have to provide for your family. Do you think I am too biased to hear this case?

PROSECUTOR No, Your Honor.

THE COURT Proceed.

Confrontation Problem

(Chris Cannon, San Francisco)

COUNSEL One minor matter, Your Honor. I raised the objection about Counsel asking if Mr. Smith relied on Dr. Oscar telling him about X, Y, and Z. Dr. Oscar is never going to testify because he is dead.

THE COURT So the government is not going to bring him back.

Gone with the Wind

(Delgado Smith, Texarkana, TX)

THE COURT I'm going to get some coffee. You guys can keep arguing. It doesn't have an effect on me.

The Imperial We Surprise

(Mario Cano, Coral Gables, FL)

THE COURT With regard to the motion by defendant for judgment of acquittal, we feel we are compelled by virtue of the evidence that has come in here to enter a judgment of acquittal for the defendant and we hereby enter the order. We think we should like to state our reasons for doing so on the record. *[Does so at length]* Having said that, Mr. Defense Counsel, we will ask you if you would be kind enough to submit an order to us entering a judgment of acquittal . . . and the marshals will at that point release your client forthwith. Mr. Marshal may take the defendant to their office at this time.

DEFENSE COUNSEL Your Honor, my client seems to have fainted.

Fast Talker

(Anonymous Bosch, New Caledonia)

THE COURT Counsel, I don't have the heart to put my staff through one more minute of your rapid speech. We're all going to take a fifteen-minute recess at this time. The student reporter is going to look for another career. I'm going to take a couple of aspirin. And you are not going to drink caffeine.

[Later to Counsel]

THE COURT You mean you're not going to be able to finish today?

COUNSEL Even at my normal speed, no.

THE COURT As you know, this is Saint Patrick's Day. And of the three attorneys, you're the only one wearing green. This is a night where you should consider raising your glass, because I understand that alcohol is a depressant.

COUNSEL If the Court is ordering me to drink tonight, I will.

THE COURT Don't put words in my mouth.

Pick the Accused

(Richard J. Krech, Oakland)

Q. And you looked at these gentlemen. You have no question in your mind that of the six gentlemen seated at this table, three of them are wearing yellow, which look like jail clothes; is that correct?

THE COURT Counsel has on a yellow tie; small bow tie but it's yellow.

Q. Of the six men that are seated here, do you have any question of which three men are in custody and which three men are lawyers?

A. No, I don't.

THE COURT That doesn't mean who should be in custody, but go ahead.

Judge Tells Jury About the Defendant

[*Quercia v. United States*, 289 U.S. 466, 468 (1933)]

And now I am going to tell you what I think of the defendant's testimony. You may have noticed, Mr. Foreman and gentlemen, that he wiped his hands during his testimony. It is rather a curious thing, but that is almost always an indication of lying. Why it should be so we don't know, but that is the fact. I think that every single word that man said, except when he agreed with the Government's testimony, was a lie.

To the Jury About Defense Counsel

[*Offutt v. United States*, 348 U.S. 11, n.3 (1954)]

I also realize that you had a difficult and a disagreeable task in this case. You have been compelled to sit through a disgraceful and disreputable performance on the part of a lawyer who is unworthy of being a member of the profession; and I, as a member of the legal profession, blush that we should have such a specimen in our midst.

The Judge on the Cop

[*Cannon v. Commission on Judicial Qualifications*, 14 Cal.3d 678 (1975)]

The judge ordered a cop hauled in off the street because he had just cautioned her about excessive horn blowing while she was driving near the courthouse. She told her bailiff: "Find the son of a bitch; I want him found and brought in right away. Give me a gun; I am going to shoot his balls off and give him a .38 vasectomy."

Leading the Witness

(Kenneth Quigley, San Francisco)

THE COURT Someone was behind you?

A. Yes.

THE COURT You didn't see him?

A. No. I didn't see him, but I feel the body behind me. And then I turned my head back, and I understand they try to get me in a circle.

DA Do you see the person you saw who was standing behind you in court today?

COUNSEL Objection, misstates the testimony. He said he didn't see him.

THE COURT Initially, he didn't see him, and then he said he turned his head and looked toward him. Is that correct?

A. First, I feel the body behind me. I feel somebody standing very close.

THE COURT Then you turned your head and looked?

A. That's right, then I—

COUNSEL Objection, leading.

THE COURT It's not leading. That is what he said.

COUNSEL Of course, you're leading.

THE COURT I'm repeating what he said.

COUNSEL Asked and answered.

THE COURT You turned your head and looked?

A. That's right.

DA And do you recognize that person in court today?

A. No.

Garbage In, Garbage Out

(Robert App, Brooklyn, NY)

COUNSEL I think we're both prepared to argue it at length.

THE COURT You both violated my cardinal rule in failing to be brief. So, that means I'm going to have to spend an hour to read this garbage. So, I'll have to hold it, and you'll have to wait for me. It's regrettable. You probably each have one case, but you gave me a plethora of garbage, and I have to read through the garbage.

PROSECUTOR We confined our argument to about four pages.

THE COURT Yours is something like sixteen pages.

COUNSEL Yes, but unfortunately, we have the burden. And we had the burden of explaining the legislative history.

THE COURT The burden doesn't take that long. When anybody sends me a big brief, I say, Oh, boy, are they in tough condition. They can't find a damn thing. They've got to put in the phone book to support their position.

COUNSEL No, Your Honor. If you'll look at those attachments to the brief.

THE COURT Attachments can be a phone book, too. The *Encyclopedia Americana.*

[Pause]

THE COURT I'm denying the motion.

PROSECUTOR We're pleased you reached the just result.

THE COURT It had nothing to do with justice.

Wait a Minute

(Mark Arnold, Bakersfield)

ORDER: Defendant's motion to prohibit the District Attorney from committing prosecutorial misconduct is denied.

Judicial Musing on Nicknames

(Maria Stratton, Los Angeles)

My name is Dick. My father's name is Dick. They used to call him big Dick. They used to call me little Dick. So, I'm not real fond of nicknames. They can be deceiving and give what may be a false sense of the person.

You Asked

(Judy Clarke, San Diego)

[The following is from a court hearing where a prosecutor examines a defense attorney about the latter's uniquely candid evaluations of the judiciary and the prosecutor]

DA Okay. The statement you made to the reporter about "I'm not going to let these cocksuckers breathe until this jumps off my ass and onto theirs," can you just be specific for me and tell me who the people are that you're referring to as cocksuckers?

COUNSEL Well, the judge, definitely, you, definitely. That will suffice for the present. That was the frame of reference, you and the judge.

Q. Are there any potential cocksuckers or possible or probable cocksuckers or people you suspect to be cocksuckers, or are we the only confirmed and adjudicated cocksuckers in the County?

A. Well, I don't know that you've been adjudicated a cocksucker yet, but you will be.

Q. Who's going to do that?

A. Well, I hope that the people who take an interest in that will find that you are a cocksucker.

Q. Who are the people that take an interest in my status as a cocksucker?

A. You'll have to ask others—that's not my game.

Q. Okay. Can you explain why you referred to the judge as a cocksucker?

A. Well, it's a term that used to describe a wretched, unethical individual. And I consider the judge unethical and wretched.

Q. The judge and myself are unethical and wretched?

A. I think you're cunning. I think you're contemptible. I think you're base. I think that you suborn perjury. Will that do for the moment? If you give me time, I can come up with a lot more. But for the present, it will have to do.

Q. What about the judge besides being a cocksucker?

A. Cocksucker—and unethical.

Q. —unethical.

Q. You've said a lot of things about me that are negative, and you're said a lot about [the other judge] that are negative. You called [the first judge] a GD liar, and you've gone into a description of why you believe him to be a liar. And I'm just asking you why isn't [the second judge] up to the level of cocksuckerdom?

A. I don't know. He may get up there soon if I nail him. But at this juncture he does not in my judgment qualify as a duly certified cocksucker.

Q. Would you say that I'm pretty much the lowest of the low and the worst that you've had to deal with?

A. You're the worst I've ever encountered.

Q. I am personally?

A. Absolutely the worst. I've seen some sleazy, slimy prosecutors in my life, but I have never seen one quite like you. You're the basest, most contemptible piece of human garbage I've ever run into. Yeah.

Q. I'm the basest and most contemptible piece of human garbage that you've ever run into?

A. No. In the criminal justice system. No, wait a second. Let me weigh that carefully. It's a photo finish. I knew one guy as bad as you. He had his wife in prostitution, and then he put two of his daughters in prostitution. He was the lowest, but God you're right in there, pal.

Q. Do you include defendants that you've represented when you're talking about me being the lowest piece of garbage that you've ever dealt with in the criminal justice system?

A. Absolutely.

Q. So you think that my conduct is even worse than murderers and drug dealers and child molesters?

A. You kill the truth.

Q. I kill the truth?

A. You kill the truth. You kill the constitutional rights of citizens. That poses a greater danger to our society

than a drug dealer or a murderer. Yes, absolutely, you're
an obscene menace.

One Reason for the Bank Bailout

(John Schuck, Palo Alto)

DEFENSE Defense would request a reduction to a misdemeanor.

DA Object.

THE COURT Although it is a lot of money, this answers some
of my questions as to why the bank industry is in such a
mess. The defendant puts an empty envelope in an ATM
with an amount stated on the envelope but no check
inside. Then he does a withdrawal from the ATM and the
bank gives it to him. Why even open the envelope if you
don't need checks inside? Because the banking industry is
at the height of stupidity and incompetence, I'm going to
grant the reduction to a misdemeanor.

Horses, Kangaroos, Lions, Tigers, Mules

[*Stevens v. Louisville*, 511 S.W.2d 228, 229–230 (Ky., 1974)]

A threshold question is presented as to whether "the ordinance
[may limit places where] horses may be ridden . . ." Appellants'
brief assaults the ordinance as being discriminatory in that it
applies only to horses as follows: "We, therefore, assume that kan-
garoo riders can employ bridle paths for their purposes but horse
riders cannot. An elephant can be ridden on the bridle path, but a
horse cannot. If a tiger could be trained, it could be ridden. Is a

donkey or a jackass a horse? What about a mule? Does this relate to live horses only or does it forbid a child rocking on a hobbyhorse? What about a mechanical horse? Could a merry-go-round be set up? The ordinance forbids none of these but only relates to the valiant steed who is such a major part of Kentucky's heritage. The trial Court's finding that this ordinance is not discriminatory because it treats all horse riders the same is misfounded. If a horse rider cannot ride his horse but can ride an animal which is not legally a horse, but similar to a horse, then the ordinance discriminates against not only the horse but the horse rider.

"Saddling the descendents of Pegasus, Man O'War, Traveler, Silver, Dan Patch, Widow Maker, Trigger, Champion, Black Beauty, Bucephalus, Rosinante, and Black Bess, to name only a few, with this asinine canon is to denigrate the legacy of the courser and the charger, the gigster and the stepper, the hunter and the racer, the clipper and the cob, the padnag and the palfrey and capitulate at last to the gasoline powered conveyance which has contributed little to our history but much to our ecological turning point."

"The Foreman will please *read* the sentence."

{ 6 }

The Jurors

When you go into court you are putting your fate into the hands of twelve people who weren't smart enough to get out of jury duty.

NORM CROSBY

A fox should not be on the jury at a goose's trial.

THOMAS FULLER

"I See Dead People"

(Howard Price, Los Angeles)

Q. Did I hear you say you're a minister?

A. Yes, I am.

Q. Did I also hear you were a spiritual minister? How did you describe yourself?

A. Spiritualist minister. And our doctrine is, we approve the continuity of life.

Q. Did I hear you say you were a medium?

A. Yes, sir.

Q. Tell me exactly what you do.

A. A medium is a connector between the living and the so-called dead. I represent dead people.

Q. Just like we see in the movies?

A. Yes, sir.

Q. Do you think any of your beliefs, philosophical or religious, however you would characterize them, would have any bearing on your deliberations in this case?

A. It makes it awkward, sir.

Q. Why do you think so?

A. Because of the fact that the deceased person would be present.

Q. In other words, you think that you could be in some sort of communication with the person that unfortunately died in this traffic accident?

A. It has happened, yes.

Q. Okay. And that would affect your ability to be fair?

A. Yes, sir.

Q. Let's say that you sit on this case. And for whatever reason—your powers, your abilities—this deceased person does try and make contact with you.

A. Yes, sir.

Q. You could not make that contact and be a fair and impartial juror.

A. True.

Q. Can you, by virtue of who you are, put a stop to that?

A. Yes, sir.

Q. Okay. Now, knowing that you'd have to, would you do that as well?

A. Yes, sir.

Q. Okay. All right. So there wouldn't be this communication, even though there's the possibility; correct?

A. Yes, sir.

Q. I thank you.

Gulp!

(Stephen Greenberg, Nevada City)

PROSPECTIVE JUROR I was on a federal jury a few months ago with methamphetamine and it didn't leave a good taste in my mouth.

Stuck-in-Time Witness

(Susan Wolk, Tarzana)

COUNSEL I notice it's almost twelve o'clock now, and I hate to jam up everybody else for lunch.

THE COURT How far do you figure?

COUNSEL I would say a good twenty minutes, Your Honor, at least. And I apologize to the Court, but the charges are serious.

THE COURT No problem. I don't want to wait that long. If it was only ten minutes, I would go ahead and do it, but I will then recess this matter until this afternoon. I'm sorry, Mr. Witness. You'll have to return at two.

WITNESS At two?

THE COURT Yes.

WITNESS Thank you. I can get down?

THE COURT No, you have to stay there till two.

Voir Dire: Fair-Minded Juror

(Jeff Harbin, Bakersfield)

Q. Do you have any bias or prejudice, either for or against the defendant because he is Hispanic?

A. No. I try to treat all criminals the same.

Hardship Excuse

(Stephen Munkelt, Nevada City)

THE COURT What we have to do is ask you those questions if you are called forward. This is only for hardship.

JUROR To me it is a hardship. I haven't had sex in over a year. I have a conjugal visit coming up. I know that sounds funny, but when you have been without it for one year, and I get called Monday morning or a Friday morning, hey, I got to be honest here.

THE COURT This is one for the books.

JUROR This is a great one for the books. It never happened to me before. I am going to have a honeymoon in a prison for white-collar-crime guys.

THE COURT By your description, it is a grave hardship.

JUROR It's been so long. Thank you. Sorry.

Voir Dire

(Delgado Smith, Texarkana, TX)

PROSPECTIVE JUROR There was a shooting at the casino. There was a big commotion because there was the sound of firearms going off and we were all crawling under the tables. We were all so scared.

THE COURT Did management of the casino or the Las Vegas Police Department take statements from you?

PROSPECTIVE JUROR No. They just took the bodies away.

THE COURT How did that affect you?

PROSPECTIVE JUROR Well, it really bummed me out, number one. I was a blackjack dealer and there was the sound of shots and I went under the table and my boss said to me, I could fire you for leaving your rack exposed. What also upset me was the fact they just got the people that were shot and the one person who committed suicide and they took them away, and they were able to come with a sweeper machine to clean the carpet and take them out of there and there was nothing to it. After that it was business as usual.

THE COURT They didn't shut down?

PROSPECTIVE JUROR No. There is no such thing. The money rules.

More Voir Dire

(Diane Nichols, Grass Valley)

Q. *[to prospective juror]* Was that your attorney?

A. That was a long time ago. I don't remember who my attorney was.

Q. Do you remember having an attorney?

A. I never had an attorney. I had a public defender.

* * *

Q. What is it in your past that gives you concern that it might make you less than a fair juror?

JUROR Well, I used to be a criminal. I've lived with criminals when I was in my twenties, and I've since been clean and sober and don't associate with criminals any longer. I was charged with a crime and convicted, and it was a misdemeanor. And I've witnessed many, many crimes because I hung out with criminals, and I did illegal drugs.

Q. Okay. When you say you were a criminal and you were convicted of a misdemeanor, was it all drug-related?

A. No. For prostitution.

* * *

THE COURT And your middle name?

WITNESS Antonio, A-N-I. I don't know. I don't even spell it.

THE COURT You can't spell your middle name?

WITNESS I don't normally use it.

* * *

Q. How did he die?

A. It was covered up. They said he woke up dead.

Laughing the Years Away

(Marti Hiken, Davis)

[During jury questioning known as voir dire]

Q. How old are you, ma'am?

A. Me?

Q. Yes.

A. I am ninety-eight.

THE COURT Ninety-eight?

WITNESS Eighty-eight.

THE COURT Eighty-eight?

WITNESS Seventy-eight.

THE COURT You just lost twenty years.

WITNESS I am sorry, I get—can't stop laughing.

THE COURT That's okay. You're doing fine.

WITNESS I am a little nervous. Your Honor, all right, I am seventy-eight.

THE COURT Thank you, you're excused.

WITNESS You're welcome.

Voir Dire

(Richard Krech, Oakland)

Q. You had mentioned earlier that you and some members of your family witnessed—did you say someone witnessed someone being killed?

A. Yeah, my first husband.

Q. Your first husband was killed?

A. Yeah.

Q. Who killed him?

A. Well, I was accused of it.

Q. Oh, I see.

A. But it was ruled accidental death, because I don't remember actually what went down, so it has been put in a sealed whatever. I don't know.

Q. I see.

A. So my attorney said it's just like more or less that it hadn't happened.

Juror's Note

(Michael Litman, San Diego)

As I sat on the panel, I noticed that one of the panel members had lice in her hair. This problem does concern me because of the epidemic it can cause to the others as well as myself. It can also become a problem for future panelists who may sit in her chair. I will leave this in your hands now, because I'm not sure about what to do.

Minute Order

(Mark Arnold, Bakersfield)

Out of the presence of the prospective jurors [Defense Counsel] moves for mistrial due to the fact that a prospective juror had "guilty" printed on a yellow sticky attached to her jury badge. Denied.

Voir Dire

(Richard Krech, Oakland)

Q. The Judge will instruct you that a defendant may choose to rely upon the state of the evidence and upon the failure, if any, of the prosecution to prove the charges beyond a reasonable doubt. Having this in mind, do you feel you could render a fair and impartial verdict if the defendant does not present any defense?

JUROR I doubt it. Why call them the defendant if they have no defense? I like to hear both sides.

Jury Verdict

(Anonymous Bosch, Paris, ID)

We the jury felt the plaintiff's closing story was insulting to us. [signed, the jurors]

Voir Dire

(Denise Kendall, Santa Cruz)

COUNSEL Now I would ask, how would you judge the credibility of somebody who gets up and sits on the stand, how are you going to judge whether you think they are telling the truth or not?

JUROR #1 By things that are presented to me, not by just their looks or actions.

JUROR #2 I'd like to say one thing. As a professional psychic, I wouldn't necessarily deal with facts. I can tell the character of someone instantly.

COUNSEL By looking at them and—

JUROR #2 Uh-huh.

COUNSEL Do you have to hear what they have to say first?

JUROR #2 No.

Voir Dire: No Problems at Home

(Sara Wilson Stander, Corte Madera)

Q. At some point in time, did you have problems that developed with your wife, marital-type problems?

A. Well, not really. We didn't have any marital problems. I just came home from work and she was gone.

Juror of Average Ignorance

(Andrew Rubin, Santa Monica)

PROSPECTIVE JUROR Yeah. Only my language, that is kind
of hard for me. I don't understand too good, and I don't
read and I don't write.

THE COURT You don't read, write, or understand? You're
quite a juror.

Jury Question (Answer: Not Yet)

(Richard Schaffer, Stockton)

[Jury Question] Does "personal property" in the definition of burglary refer to actual physical items? I.e., does theft of "peace of mind"
or other related psychological intangibles constitute burglary?

Bald DA Meets Counterculture Juror

(Jerry Blank, San Diego)

DA You seem from some of your comments before to be
somebody who has a pretty good sense of humor. I hope
you're not offended by this. You know that the makeup of
the individual personalities of people on a jury can often
have a significant effect on the outcome of cases.

JUROR Uh-huh.

DA I don't want to say there's a profile, but I think probably a
general rule in my office is that we usually don't look

favorably on prospective jurors with green hair, and we don't see that many, really. And do you have any feeling that because you, in the way you dress and your appearance, that you might have difficulty talking with a group of eleven other strangers about what you heard and what's true and not?

JUROR I would be a 9.5 on the defense's fairness scale. Try stuttering, having blue hair and shaving your legs—I ride a bike, so I get road rash—and try walking down the street and not being fair. I mean, having green hair is, I would imagine, very similar to having an elegant ring of hair, as I notice you have.

Jury Questionnaire

(John N. Aquilina, Riverside)

Q. Why do you hold the opinion that you do regarding the death penalty?

A. I am not in favor or against it because I think each case has different circumstances. I feel if you are found guilty of a serious crime where you take someone's life, you should be punished by the death penalty. If you are found not guilty, you should not be punished by the death penalty.

Voir Dire

(Mike Crain, Los Angeles)

Q. What is your reason for being excused?

A. Bluntly, I hate courts. They are responsible for rape and murders in the United States. The gas station attendant where I used to do business was murdered in a robbery. That was the fourth one. I'm getting sick and tired of the way you guys run this place. The Warren Court ruined this country.

Q. Where would you like to live? I will be glad to buy you a ticket. Would you like to go to Russia?

A. I want to live here.

Q. Would you like to go to Cuba? I will buy you a ticket anyplace you want to go, if you don't like it here.

A. I just don't like the way the lousy Warren Court ruined this country.

THE COURT You are excused.

Good Advice

(David Stanley, Sacramento)

PROSPECTIVE JUROR A As a schoolteacher in Pomona, I've had a number of students killed. Some are the shooters and some are the victims. Personally, my house has been broken into five times. My car has been hit and run, and a man died of multiple stab wounds on my lawn last September.

PROSPECTIVE JUROR B Time to move.

Sex Charge with Foreign Object

(Anonymous Bosch, Paris, ID)

PROSPECTIVE JUROR What is a foreign object? Because it would seem that some foreign objects could be pleasurable and some could not.

COUNSEL I think perhaps we should approach the bench before I respond to that.

The Chosen One

(Kelvin D. Filer, Compton)

JUROR My children are—my wife and I, we're separated. My wife was involved with an incest thing. When I found out, the mother of my children—incest, and the next seven months, the doctor tried to talk to her. And when she left, that's when I found out this happened. And a spirit came upon us, and she was talking—we fight a lot. That's when I found out about it because of the argument. After a while she started—a spirit came upon us on the fireplace. And the spirit is from God. And he told me I'm the chosen one. And I'm not crazy. I'm not crazy. I went to a Jewish rabbi. I went to a Catholic priest. He starts getting mad at me as soon as I mentioned the spirit. I went to a Christian priest, a minister. I prove each and every one of them wrong. I used to work and sued them for one billion dollars, but they got so scared they quickly settled out of court for seventy-three million. I called the FBI. They told me it's been settled out of court.

Perfect Juror

(J. Frank McCabe, San Francisco)

THE COURT May there be a stipulation that Miss Z., who is constantly and currently undergoing psychotherapy, who was released from the hospital after an eight-day stay in a mental institution, mental ward, be excused for cause?

COUNSEL I insist that we bring her in, Your Honor.

CO-COUNSEL I'll join. Normally people in that position can be expected to approach this task in a more rational fashion than any other.

Juror Projectile

(Richard Krech, Oakland)

Q. You mentioned that it may be hard to be objective in your questionnaire because of the charges.

A. Yes, that's right.

Q. What do you mean by that?

A. Because I can't listen—I can't listen to the explanation of certain things.

Q. When you say you can't, are you telling us—

A. It might make me throw up.

Q. I'm sure juror #7 will . . .

A. She might not like that, I'm sure.

Juror Hardship Request—Granted!

(Lois Katz, San Francisco)

JUROR Last winter, I blew a hole in my anus and that hole became infected. The doctors at the hospital had to cut a canal into that area so it could drain. That canal is still draining and will continue to drain for some time. Sitting for long periods is painful and messy. The areas (one inch from the anus opening) needs cleaning every two hours or so.

Voir Dire

(William Dow III, New Haven, CT)

Q. You got probation and a suspended sentence. Tell me how you thought you were treated in that case, fairly or unfairly?

JUROR Shitty. Flat out.

Juror Note to Court

(Judy Clarke, San Diego)

[This is from a trial in North Carolina; the spelling errors are those of the juror]

Your honor, I am tired of spending day after day wasting my time listening to this bullcrap. This is cruel and unusal punishment. The plantif is an idiot. He has no case. Why are we here? I think my cat could better anser these questions. And he wouldn't keep asking to see a document. I've been patient. I've sat in these chairs for 7 days now. If I believed for a second this was going to end on Thursday I might not go crazy. This is going to last for another 4 weeks. I cannot take this. I hate these lawyers and prayed one would die so the case would end. I shouldn't be on this jury. I want to die. I don't want to be thanked for my patience. I want to die! Well not die for real but that is how I feel sitting here. I am the judge, you've said that over and over. Well, I am not fair and balanced. I hate the plantif. His ignorance is driving me crazy. I know I'm writing this in vain but I have to do something . . . for my sanity. These jury chairs should come with a straight jacket. And entire day today and we are still on the same witness. The defense hasn't even started yet and we have 3 days left. 3 days my ass. Not that the defense needs a turn considering the plantif and his lawyer (who looks like the Penguin) have no case!!!! Thanks for letting me get this off my chesk. Please keep the disordelies nearby. I may need them. Juror #5.

Sad Practice, Perfectly Excusable

(Peter Scalisi, Riverside)

THE COURT Is there any reason, whether it be moral, religious or philosophical, why you cannot or do not want to be a juror in this trial?

JUROR This probably applies to the "moral." I am an alcoholic.

THE COURT Okay.

JUROR I require a certain amount of alcohol every day to get by.

THE COURT All right. So you are not a recovering alcoholic?

JUROR No. I am practicing.

THE COURT You know, they have places that can help you.

JUROR Yes, sir. If I wanted help.

THE COURT Well, that's the first step, isn't it?

JUROR Yes, sir.

THE COURT And that might interfere with your sitting as a juror?

JUROR I am sure it would. I become very antsy.

Jury Note: Mop Up Time

(Rebecca Jones, San Diego)

Eleven guilty, 1 undecided. We cannot reach unanimous vote. We 11 do not want to let it go undecided. [signed] Floor person.

A Prosecutor's Favorite Juror

(J. Courtney Shevelson, Monterey)

DA Would you be willing to acquit the defendants if I fail in my burden of proof?

PROSPECTIVE JUROR You're going to have to really screw up to get me to vote against you, partner. Because I believe that you would not come in this court unless you had all your ducks in a row. And their [defense] job is to say anything to get their people off.

Juror Questioning

(Knut Johnson, San Diego)

Q. Is there anything you would like to bring to the Court's attention that might in any way affect your ability to be a fair and impartial juror in this case?

JUROR 1 I am frequently clairvoyant. I think that might contaminate the process.

JUROR 2 I like the "A.B." [Aryan Brotherhood]. I am white and I would join their organization. I am racist and I support Aryans and other whites.

Q. Is there anything about the charges that might bias you?

JUROR 2 They are already in prison. Let them kill each other off! Who cares if a prisoner kills another loser prisoner.

Head Count

(J. Frank McCabe, San Francisco)

THE COURT What's the problem with the other juror?

JUROR Yesterday he threatened to knock me down and prior to that he's slowly escalated with touching, feeling, saying he likes little women; he can do a lot for them. He places his feet in front of me so I have to step over him. He does very strange things in the jury room. He has a penchant for swatting flies and lining their little bodies up on a paper towel next to me and counts them and has everyone look at them.

Urge to Serve

(J. Frank McCabe, San Francisco)

COUNSEL And first of all, I'm going to excuse Juror #10. Thank you very much.

THE COURT That being the case, the alternate next order, and that would be Alternate #2, will now become Juror #10.

ALTERNATE #2 Is that me?

THE COURT That is you.

ALTERNATE #2 Oh, horse hockey. I was going to get my hair done today.

Prosecution Juror

(Chuck Weisselberg, Berkeley)

THE COURT The Court once had a juror who said he believed in the death penalty in all cases where the defendant was guilty, but he also believed in life without parole if they were not guilty. And the Court requestioned him, and the juror was from Jordan and he had a Mideast view on justice. He said not guilty means no penalty, and the juror held to his position that if someone is arrested, they should have life without parole. So he was excused by the Court although the DA stood up and said he'd like twelve more just like him.

Identity Crisis

(Josh Needle, Santa Monica)

[Jury Question of the Court]
We, the jury in this case, submit the following request or question to the Court: Is the defense attorney an attorney or a public defender?

Jury Lottery

(J. Frank McCabe, Burlingame)

THE COURT My law clerk brought to my attention that on the way out in the last recess you gave her a note that says, "Do you want to play in our lottery? It's only a dollar." I need to understand what lottery you are talking about.
JUROR The California lottery. The Mega Millions.
THE COURT What's going on? You're going to put that in the California lottery? And then what happens if you win?
JUROR We split it all with the people who put into it.

Juror Voir Dire

(Courtney Shevelson, Monterey)

PROSPECTIVE JUROR I have four jobs at the moment. I'm part time at Pet Food Express. I just got bonded as a process server. I play video games professionally, and I'm site manager for my dad's company. I have never served on a jury. I was arrested over the weekend. A few friends and I had been drinking and we went streaking and got caught.

They didn't press charges because they thought it was really funny. They made us put our clothes on. As to being fair and impartial, I know both of the defendants just seeing them around at parties. I don't personally know them. I've held conversations with them at parties. I've seen them. And I know them personally. I'd rather see them on the street than in jail. Like, that is just where I would be.

THE COURT You're excused.

DEFENSE COUNSEL *[to juror]* Do you want my card?

JUROR Sure.

THE COURT He's kidding.

JUROR I'm going to need it soon enough.

Model Juror

(Hon. Runston Maino, Vista)

THE COURT Juror #25, tell us about yourself.

JUROR You talk about experiences with the law. I alluded to criminal investigations. I alluded to domestic violence. I also alluded to I have an education in law. I've also written law. I had numerous attempts on my life throughout my life. I've been accused of committing domestic violence. I have been accused of numerous things.

I have been investigated. I never been convicted. I have gone to court on a murder one charge. I have gone to court, grand jury, a couple of them. I've never been convicted of a felony. I have been charged with just about everything. I've worked with good judicial systems and I've worked with the bad. I worked with good police offi-

cers and I worked with bad ones. I work with good pre-
cincts and bad ones. You asked for litigations—and won
for various things.

THE COURT Do you think you can be fair to both sides?

JUROR Yes, I can. I'll give you a prime example what I have
done in the past. Somebody attempted to murder me. We
took them to court. They were prosecuted. They got by
with it. We had films, overwhelming evidence. These
people, the jury was blind. Then it wasn't a week later
after the trial which lasted three weeks that the three
came at it again except this time we had the man who
ordered the hit. He was caught, put him on trial. The
three that came out to murder me were killed by the federal authorities. The person we put on trial who ordered
the hit was going to die soon, and I was on the stand and
giving my testimony and went through a hard day. The
doctor told him to give him one nitroglycerin. I pulled the
pills out and gave him two and requested the judge that
we just don't have the trial. He'll be dead in a few days
anyway. Then he asked me why I gave the nitroglycerin
tablets. I told him because I don't care who he is, what he's
accused of. Every person has a right to a fair trial no matter
how guilty. And there again, we had overwhelming evidence, and although I agree for the defense's side, I have
been aggressive toward a woman. She was a pedophile. She
was in there incarcerated. She was lifting 250-pound
weights. That was self-defense. She had a firm grip, a hold
of my hand, and I hit her with the other one for the release,
and that was all. I might have hit her two or three times.

When the aggression stopped, I stopped. That was investigated, but I have been investigated numerous times for different things. Never convicted.

Hard Way to Get Out of Jury Service

(John N. Aquilina, Riverside)

THE COURT Deputy, I understand you're requesting two potential jurors be excused?

DEPUTY Yes, Your Honor.

THE COURT My understanding is that one of these jurors stole another juror's purse?

DEPUTY Yes, Your Honor.

Voir Dire: Juror Bottom Line

(William F. Dow III, New Haven, CT)

Q. I want to ask you about that and I know the Judge asked you some questions and all I want is your honest answer. Okay? Do you feel that your situation, your feelings, are going to be such that if you feel the State has proven its case beyond a reasonable doubt, you're just going to say, Jees, I'd like to say he's guilty, I believe the State's proven it, but I can't say that. Are you going to have that situation?

A. I can say that because, like I said, it's not my ass.

Einstein's Theory of Relative Doubt

(Domenic Lombardo, San Diego)

[Jury Note] In a court of law, which equation best represents how reasonable doubt (Y) is to be evaluated?

1. Y='s A (felon) + B (gun) + C (chase) + D (ran) + E (knew), or

2. Y='s A (felon) x B (gun) x C (chase) x D (ran) x E (knew)

Clothes Make the Man

(David Carleton, Los Angeles)

PROSPECTIVE JUROR The other item is the defendant's appearance. How do I say this? It looks to me like he's wearing a disguise. Normally folks wearing suits and a dress shirt don't wear white socks, and that tells me that perhaps he's disguising his normal appearance, and I should have mentioned that, too, I guess.

THE COURT Counsel, do you have any questions?

COUNSEL Can you think of any other reason why my client might be wearing white socks?

PROSPECTIVE JUROR Perhaps you made a mistake dressing him.

"I misspoke—I meant lousy liar, not lying louse."

{ 7 }

Malaprops

I have kleptomania, but when it gets bad, I take something for it.

ANON

Suicidal twin kills sister by mistake!

ANON

My uncle's dying wish was to have me sitting in his lap;
he was in the electric chair.

RODNEY DANGERFIELD

Clothes Make the Man

(Samuel Eaton, Jr., Santa Barbara)

DA Do you know the defendant?

A. Yes, I do.

DA Do you see him in Court today?

A. Yes, I do.

DA How is he dressed?

A. He looks pretty sharp.

Worker's Compensation

(Patricia Fox, Sunnyvale)

Q. And is what you told the police the truth that night?

A. Yes, it was.

Q. And what do you recall the nature of the threats?

A. Well, I'm pretty sure he said he would kill me. And then he told me to give him oral compensation.

Q. He hold you what?

A. Oral compensation. He pulled his pants down and said to do that like I did to the man next door.

Ethyl's Dead Drunk

(David McGlaughlin, Philadelphia)

Q. And, in fact, going over to the certificate of analysis that is provided to the Court and myself, we see that the

Guth Laboratories have found that the simulator solution in this particular lot number contains .1207 lethal alcohol?

A. Correct.

Beastly Criminal Charges

(Ken Quigley, San Francisco)

Count 4: that the said defendant(s), in the city and county of San Francisco, state of California, committed the crime of felony, to wit: violating the California Penal Code, in that the said defendant(s) did willfully and unlawfully, for gain, hire, reward and gratuitously record and register bets and wagers upon the result of a purported contest of skill, speed, and power of endurance between *beasts,* to wit: professional and college basketball games, baseball games.

Don't Know Jack?

(Gerald V. Scotti, Beverly Hills)

[From DA argument to the jury]

The defendant tells the other guy that he'll provide backup. He'll provide protection. His people will be there. You will hear him say on the tape that he jacks people. And you will hear testimony from officers as to what "jack" means. "Jack" is when you rip somebody off, when you jack someone off.

Who's on First?

(Marcia Levine, Truckee)

Q. Despite having ten or eleven beers before you went, you were sober enough to drive from Trouble's house to the 7-Eleven?

A. Right.

Q. You didn't have trouble driving your car?

A. I did but I didn't crash.

Q. I'm sorry?

THE COURT "Trouble" with a big "T."

Q. You didn't have David, known as Trouble, drive your car for you?

A. No.

Q. You didn't know how many beers he had and you knew you had eleven?

A. About there, ten or eleven, yes.

Q. You did have trouble driving your car but you just didn't crash?

A. No.

Q. I'm sorry. Did I not understand what you just said?

COUNSEL The question is compound. He said no, he didn't crash.

DA I'll rephrase it.

Q. Did you have trouble driving your car?

A. No, nobody drove my car.

Q. Okay. Now we are back to the other problem. Now I am not referring to David. I'm referring to the adjective. Did you have difficulty, or trouble, just difficulty, driving your car?

A. Not really.

Man (Not So) Well

(Michael J. Oliver, Pleasant Hill)

THE COURT You care to address any issue?

COUNSEL It's less than a gram of methamphetamine. Doesn't seem to really fairly be charged as a felony. As I cited previously, the Manwell Noriega rule says only Manwell Noriega ought to be held to answer for a felony regarding less than a gram of methamphetamine.

Hand Job

(David P. Carleton, Los Angeles)

Q. Revolvers, do they eject shell casings from the cylinder or not?

A. They do not.

Q. I mean, automatically ejaculate.

A. They do not. They have to do it by hand after moving the cylinder out of the frame.

Murder Case Repartee

(George Schraer, San Diego)

COUNSEL Your Honor, at this point it is my position that I will not inquire about the 1979 conviction unless there appears to be additional chicanery on the part of this witness.

THE COURT So pending a chicanery hearing, we won't mention that.

Instruction: Oral Emission

(George Schraer, San Diego)

An emission is a statement made by the defendant other than at his trial which does not by itself acknowledge his guilt of the crimes for which such defendant is on trial. But, which statement tends to prove his guilt when considered with the rest of the evidence.

Refreshed

(David P. Carleton, Los Angeles)

Q. How many kilograms were in the boxes in the garage?

A. I can't recall the exact number.

Q. Would it refresh your recollection to take a look at page 5 of a Department of Justice report?

A. Yes, it might.

Q. Drawing your attention to a specific area—

A. I have never seen that report before.

Q. Does that refresh your erection, however?

A. As to how many kilos were in the garage?

THE COURT You mean refresh your recollection?

Q. Freudian slip. Yes, sir.

Small Yards, Big Feet

(Maureen De Mais, Santa Barbara)

Q. And how far from you to the man with the gun?

A. He wasn't any further, not even 10 yards. He was probably about 10 yards behind me.

Q. About 30 feet then?

A. Right.

Q. From you. Okay. If you could write 30 feet.

A. No, not 30 feet. About 10 yards. He's 10 yards.

Q. Okay.

A. 30 feet is a lot further than 10 yards.

Latin Preference

(Neil Morse, San Francisco)

DEFENSE COUNSEL And then the defense?

THE COURT It's the Court's practice to start with the prosecution, and I would ask the D.A. to voir-dire the jury *ad seriatim.*

DEFENSE COUNSEL Would you run that by me again?

THE COURT *Ad seriatim.*

DEFENSE COUNSEL I'm sorry. All at once? One at a time?

THE COURT That means one, two, three, four, five, six, seven, eight, nine, ten . . .

DEFENSE COUNSEL One through twelve?

THE COURT Yes, in that order, not bouncing around, *ad seri-*

atim. And that means, when he's done, you can ask your questions *ad seriatim.*

DEFENSE COUNSEL I'd prefer to ask them *ad nauseam,* if you don't mind.

What About PU?

(Anonymous Bosch, Paris, ID)

DEFENSE COUNSEL Your Honor, the next exhibit number we have is BO. Any objection if I eliminated BO and went to the next one?

THE COURT Whatever you want to do.

WITNESS You might skip BS also.

COUNSEL Good point. Thank you. And I will.

Current Flame

(George Schraer, San Diego)

Q. How do you know Robert?

A. He used to be my ex-boyfriend.

Defamation

(Delgado Smith, Texarkana, TX)

DA Good morning, ma'am.

A. Good morning.

Q. You are married to the defendant's husband, correct?

DEFENSE COUNSEL I have to object.

WITNESS I hope not.

DEFENSE COUNSEL I object to character assassination. Big-
amy is a crime in this state.

DA You know what I mean.

THE COURT No, I don't know what you mean.

Q. Your relationship with the defendant is . . .

A. My relationship with the defendant is that she is my
sister-in-law. She is married to my brother.

Semantics

(Gregory B. English, Alexandria, VA)

Q. Isn't it true that you have voluntarily performed consen-
sual fellatio upon my client many times in the past?

A. I don't know what that means but I done gave him a ton of
blow jobs.

Off and On

(Gregory B. English, Alexandria, VA)

[From an arrest warrant] The complainant stated that the defendant
and her have five children in common and had been dating on and
off for six years.

Sliming Down the Case

(Eric Multhaup, Mill Valley)

DA Your Honor, this might come as a shock to the defense,
but our hope is that we get our case done in two months.
We're in the process of sliming down our case.

Not Suitable for Probation

(Charles Bonneau, Sacramento)

THE COURT This is a case where the defendant is not sartorially eligible for probation. Even if he were, he would not be a suitable candidate for probation.

Police Report: The Position

(James M. Baw, Merced)

The victim stated that she willingly had sex with the suspect and that they only had sex one time in the usual military position.

Do You Have a Psychopathic Probation Officer?

(Delgado Smith, Texarkana)

Cal Wel & Inst Code §6779 reads: "Wherever in this code or in any other statute reference is made to psychopathic probation officers, such reference shall be deemed to mean and refer to the counselors in mental health provided for in this chapter. . . ."

Imployee Wantid with Languidge Skils

(Al Menaster, Los Angeles)

[From an ad for new Public Defenders]

"The services provided by the Public Defender is mandated under federal law . . . Typical Dutie . . ."

Route en Route

(George Schraer, San Diego)

THE COURT Next witness.

COUNSEL #1 The next witness is en route, Your Honor.

THE COURT That's an odd name.

COUNSEL #2 First initial "n."

COUNSEL #1 En route will be here momentarily.

Crappy and Hard of Hearing

(J. Frank McCabe, Burlingame)

A. The only discussions we had about testifying is because I had been through this before. And I had just basically told them, when you go in there just be honest, you know. And just pay attention to some of these crafty defense lawyers that are trying to twist you up.

Q. These crappy ones? Who told you that, your crappy defense attorney?

A. Not crappy. Crafty.

Motion to Strike Impertinent and Scandalous Matter

(Phil Schnayerson, Hayward)

Plaintiff, by her attorneys, hereby moves this Court to strike as impertinent and scandalous the characterization of her factual submission as "dreck." As grounds therefore, plaintiff states:

1. For almost four years now, plaintiff and her attorneys have been subjected to the constant kvetching by defendants' counsel, who have made a big tsimmes about the quantity and quality of plaintiff's responses to discovery requests. This has been the source of much tsoris among plaintiff's counsel and a big megillah for the Court.

2. Now that plaintiff's counsel has, after much time and effort, provided defendants with a specific and comprehensive statement of plaintiff's claims and the factual basis thereof, defendants' counsel have the chutzpah to call it "dreck" and to urge the Court to ignore it.

3. Plaintiff moves that this language be stricken for several reasons. First, we think it is impertinent to refer to the work of a fellow member of the bar of this Court with the Yiddish term "dreck" as it would be to use "the sibilant four-letter English word for excrement." Rosten, *The Joys of Yiddish* (New York: Simon & Schuster, 1968), p. 103. Second, defendants are in no position to deprecate plaintiff's counsel in view of the chozzerai which they have filed over the course of this litigation. Finally, since not all of plaintiff's lawyers are yeshiva bochurs, defendants should not have assumed that they would all be conversant in Yiddish.

Wherefore, plaintiff prays that the Court put an end to the mishegoss and strike "dreck."

Sliced and Diced

(Kim Malcheski, San Francisco)

[Police report] The witness knows this older subject as "Jom Gai" ("Chopped Chicken"), so called because he has been stabbed many times in fights.

Rainbow Coalition

(Diana Samuelson, Sacramento)

Q. Were you aware of the races of the deputies involved?

A. Pardon me.

Q. In the lawsuit.

A. Pardon me.

Q. Were you aware of the races of the deputies involved in the lawsuit?

A. What do you mean races?

Q. Black, White, Hispanic, Oriental, anything else you can think of.

A. To my knowledge it's all racists.

Always Never Forget, Always Never Forget

(Jack Campbell, Vista)

THE COURT Never forget, Counsel, this is a court of redundancy.

COUNSEL Your Honor, I will always never forget this is a

court of redundancy. Your Honor, I will always never forget this is a court of redundancy.

Tasteless Voir Dire

(Ronald Dreifort, Corning)

JUROR Our house was broken into.

Q. How long ago was that?

A. Twenty years.

Q. Was there an investigation done?

A. Yes.

Q. Did they find anybody?

A. Yes, it was a neighbor kid.

Q. It usually is.

Q. Was there a prosecution?

A. No.

Q. Okay. I take it you settled without that?

A. Yes.

Q. Did you get your property back?

A. No, they ate part of it.

Q. Any bad taste left in your mouth from that?

Grand Jury Witless

(Michael Chaney, Los Angeles)

Q. Another grand juror asks if you were given a grant of
immunity in order to come here and testify today?

A. I don't understand that—immunity?

Q. Is it fair to say that you have never discussed immunity with the District Attorney?

A. What does immunity mean? Does that mean they are going to give me money or something? I don't understand. I'm not very smart.

Sinking Discovery

(Earl Bute, New York City)

DA The status of the boat has no relevance to this case at all. This is a total fishing expedition.

Police Report: Indecent Exposure

(Carol Strickman, Oakland)

Officer West arrived obscene at 1342 hours and at my direction interviewed the suspect.

The Police

{ 8 }

The Police

An illegal alien in Polk County Florida who got pulled over in a routine traffic stop ended up "executing" the deputy who stopped him. The deputy was shot eight times, including once behind his right ear at close range. Another deputy was wounded and a police dog killed. A statewide manhunt ensued.

The murderer was found hiding in a wooded area and as soon as he took a shot at the SWAT team, officers opened fire on him. They hit the guy 68 times.

Naturally, the liberal media went nuts and asked why they had to shoot the poor undocumented immigrant 68 times.

Sheriff Grady Judd told the Orlando Sentinel: "Because that's all the ammunition we had." Now, is that just about the all-time greatest answer or what!

The Coroner also reported that the illegal alien died of natural causes. When asked by a reporter how that could be since there were 68 bullet wounds in his body, he simply replied, "When you are shot 68 times you are naturally gonna die."

Miranda Rights: Dead on Arrival

(Charles Bonneau, Sacramento)

OFFICER Your Honor, after reading him his last rites I explained to him. . . .

THE COURT Not his last rites. You read him his constitutional rights.

OFFICER Okay.

Takes One to Know One

(Anonymous Bosch, Paris, ID)

The defendant was one of the three males that I saw. He was out of breath, had a bloody lip, and didn't speak very well English.

Too Many Doughnuts

(Marylou Hillberg, Santa Rosa)

Q. Is it common for you to work with people who are involved in drugs as undercover informants?

A. Absolutely.

Q. Why?

A. I can't buy dope, Counsel. I don't have the figure for it. I don't have the age for it. Deputy Charles probably would be the best one in our office to buy dope because he's young enough and he's slender enough. The rest of us are all old fat cops and we're well known. The only way we catch people actually selling it is if they're just terminally stupid and they do it right in front of us. Absent that, every other case that we do involves an undercover informant of some sort.

DUI Report

(Joan L. Pantsios, Wheaton, IL)

I asked the suspect to do some field sobriety tests. Tests were performed in a parking lot. He said he would have a hard time doing the tests because he was a high school dropout.

Plain View

(Hon. Steven J. Howell, Oroville)

I am a police officer with the city of Chico. I was on duty and initiated a traffic stop on a vehicle near C St. and E. 16th St. The vehicle did not display a rear license plate. I contacted the female passenger and saw a hypodermic syringe in her bra. The syringe was in plain view.

Pizza Craze

(Christopher Cannon, San Francisco)

[The following is a direct quote from the Center for Strategic and International Studies Report on Global Organized Crime; the author who introduces the story swears it's true]

FBI agents conducted a raid of a psychiatric hospital in San Diego that was under investigation for medical insurance fraud. After hours of reviewing thousands of medical records, the dozens of agents had worked up quite an appetite. The agent in charge of the investigation called a nearby pizza parlor with delivery service to order a quick dinner for his colleagues. The following telephone conversation took place and was recorded by the FBI because they were taping all conversations at the hospital.

AGENT [A] Hello. I would like to order 19 large pizzas and 67 cans of soda.

PIZZA MAN [PM] And where would you like them delivered?

A. We're over at the psychiatric hospital.

PM. The psychiatric hospital?

A. That's right. I'm an FBI agent.

PM. You're an FBI agent?

A. That's correct. Just about everybody here is.

PM. And you're at the psychiatric hospital?

A. That's correct. And make sure you don't go through the front doors. We have them locked. You will have to go around to the back to the service entrance to deliver the pizzas.

PM. And you say you're all FBI agents?

A. That's right. How soon can you have them here?

PM. And everyone at the psychiatric hospital is an FBI agent?

A. That's right. We've been here all day and we're starving.

PM. How are you going to pay for all of this?

A. I have my checkbook right here.

PM. And you're all FBI agents?

A. That's right. Everyone here is an FBI agent. Can you remember to bring the pizzas and sodas to the service entrance in the rear? We have the front doors locked.

PM. I don't think so. [click]

Affidavit for Truthful Liar

(Michael Thorman, Hayward)

"X" is a confidential reliable informant. "X" has also provided information that led to the seizure of controlled substances on at least two occasions. "X" has also provided information about controlled substance traffickers, which I have found to be true and accurate on at least two occasions. I request the Court assume for the purpose of the affidavit that "X" is either on probation or parole, and "X" has suffered at least one prior felony conviction. "X" has a prior arrest and conviction for providing false information to a police officer, but this arrest/conviction was prior to the at least two occasions that "X" has provided accurate information to the police. "X" has a pending criminal case and has been promised consideration in return for providing this information. No other compensation, inducements, or promises have been given to "X."

Identity Crisis

(Charles Feer, Bakersfield)

Q. What happened when you first made contact with the defendant? What did you do after he turned and you came together?

A. I once again told myself I was a police officer and that I was investigating marijuana growth.

Police Version of Truth

(Eugene Iredale, San Diego)

Q. But when you said that, it was your intention never to talk to my [defense] investigator, right?

A. Correct.

Q. Because it's your standing policy not to talk to defense investigators, right?

A. Yes, sir.

Q. You're a policeman and you're on the side of the DA, and that's it, right?

A. No, sir, I'm not on anybody's side.

Q. You're here to tell the truth.

A. Yes, sir.

Q. And only the truth.

A. Yes, sir.

Q. And nothing but the truth.

A. Yes, sir.

Q. That's why you talk to one side of the case, but not the other, right?

A. Yes, sir.

California Highway Patrol: Safety First

(Tom McGuire, Tulare)

Q. Now, this comment you made yesterday that you used the driver as a shield, there is no mention of that in your police report, is there?

A. No.

Q. And you didn't make any mention of that at the preliminary hearing?

A. No. I wasn't asked.

Q. Is it California Highway Patrol standard operating procedure to use civilians as human shields?

A. It is hard to say—

Q. How long have you been a police officer, sir?

A. Thirty-one years, twenty-nine in the Highway Patrol and two on the city.

Q. In those thirty-one years, how many times have you personally used a human as a shield?

A. A couple hundred times.

Miranda Waiver by Poor Posture

(Max B. De Lima, Laguna Hills)

[Police Report] When the sergeant and I began questioning the defendant in detail about the handgun he stole and later sold, he stopped answering and said he should speak with an attorney. At that point, I told him I would stop asking him about the gun and how he disposed of it. He nodded his head in agreement and moved his body forward. This movement was indicative to one "being open to more questioning." I asked him if I could ask about other burglaries and he nodded his head "yes." Without mentioning this previous burglary, I then began to ask him about several other burglaries I had been investigating.

In the Bag

(Jerry Shuford, Indio)

[*Police Report*] I began to search the pickup truck, and I paid most attention to the driver's side bed of the pickup truck. I saw that the bed was half filled with grass. I looked in the direction where I had seen the defendant reaching for something. I saw a brown and beige plastic bag (Albertson's shopping bag) with a knot in it. This bag appeared to be the size similar to a shoe box. I initially thought that the methamphetamine I was looking for was possibly in this bag. I cut the bag open and found it to contain cold tamales. I was slightly disappointed.

The Inference

(Richard Krech, Oakland)

[*Police Report*] I admonished defendant. As I read the admonishment she kept repeating "fuck you." I interpreted this as that she did not wish to give a statement at this time.

A Matter of Feline Delicacy

(Ken Quigley, San Francisco)

Q. You asked him what he was doing?
A. Yeah.
Q. What did he tell you?
A. That he was trying to get laid or trying to get some. He was trying to get laid.

Q. Were you just being delicate with your language by pausing there at "trying to get some."

A. Yeah.

Q. Okay. Could you please tell us the exact words?

A. If I can refer to the reports so I don't get it wrong. I am remembering it in my head, but I don't want to be misquoted.

Q. I wouldn't do that. Okay. Please refer to your report, whatever you need to do.

A. I wrote in quotes, "so I can get laid."

Q. As far as you can remember was that the exact quote, then?

A. If I remember correctly there was more to it, but I put in the initial statement.

Q. Well, out of a sense of delicacy, there was a reference to a small cat that you omitted from your report?

A. Yeah.

DEA Letter to Defense Counsel: Free Samples

(Paul Potter, Pasadena)

Pursuant to Title 21 U.S.C. §881 (f) (2), the Drug Enforcement Administration (DEA) intends to destroy the bulk of the drug evidence seized from the 1984 Oldsmobile. As I informed you over the telephone, you may view and/or sample the drug evidence within 14 days from the date of this letter. After that time, the evidence will be destroyed.

Touché

(Anonymous Bosch, Paris, ID)

Q. Officer, did you see my client fleeing the scene?

A. No, sir. But I subsequently observed a person matching the description of the offender, running several blocks away.

Q. Officer, who provided this description?

A. The officer who responded to the scene.

Q. A fellow officer provided the description of this so-called offender. Do you trust your fellow officers?

A. Yes, sir. With my life.

Q. With your life? Let me ask you this, then, Officer. Do you have a room where you change your clothes in preparation for your daily duties?

A. Yes, sir, we do.

Q. And do you have a locker in the room?

A. Yes, sir, I do.

Q. And do you have a lock on your locker?

A. Yes, sir.

Q. Now why is it, Officer, if you trust your fellow officers with your life, you find it necessary to lock your locker in a room you share with these same officers?

A. You see, sir, we share the building with the court complex, and sometimes lawyers have been known to walk through that room.

Keeping It Real

(Ken Quigley, San Francisco)

[Police interrogation of suspect]

Q. Well, we're just trying to see if you're responsible for it.

A. I'm not, so I'm not tripping. And I know I ain't done shit in this county so there's no point in me even talking to you guys. It doesn't make any sense.

Q. You don't have to. You and I are done. If you want to talk to Tom, you can talk to Tom.

A. I don't want to talk to Tom. I don't want to talk to anybody really. I shouldn't even really talk to you because I know I haven't done anything and I haven't even been over here. Period. So what am I doing here?

Q. I'm trying to clear your good name.

A. I don't have a good name. Let's keep it real, okay?

Memories of an Undercover Cop

(Howard Price, Beverly Hills)

Q. You also indicated in addition to the 821 arrests I just referred to, that you assisted additionally in 5,287 narcotic arrests; is that correct?

A. Yes, actually it's 5,682 now.

Q. All right. So just as of the date of this incident, going back to August of last year, between your own personal arrests, 821, and the 5,287 that you assisted in, would that be over the eleven years and eight months that you referred to?

A. No, that actually would be four years and seven months.

Q. So, in other words, in four years you either arrested personally or assisted in the arrests of 6,180 people?

A. No. That's 5,682, sir. You just gave me some more bodies that I haven't touched yet.

Q. Let me understand your report. You did say that you made 821 arrests?

A. Yes. That 821 arrests also includes that total, that round total, that 5,000.

Q. So the 821 is included in the 5,287?

A. That's correct, sir.

Q. Then my question is that 5,287 arrests that you participated in was over a four-year period?

A. That's correct.

Q. Do you work 365 days a year?

A. Do we? No. Do you?

COUNSEL I do, yes. I'm a defense lawyer.

Q. So whatever period of time you actually worked over a four-year period, if we divided that number into this 5,287, we would find out how many arrests per day you made, correct?

A. No, that would be incorrect, because we are an undercover buy team. That's what we do; we go out and buy narcotics from street dealers. During that time we were working upwards to five to six days a week. So my team in that week time we can arrest almost thirty to forty people. And it's not just one officer going out and buying. We have got eight operating. And sometimes we arrest upwards of five people at a time.

Q. I'm just trying to understand what you are saying.

A. Well, what you are trying to get me to lock down. I cannot give you facts of what you are asking without me going over it.

Q. I'm not trying to lock you down. I'm just trying to understand that you are saying in a four-year period, you personally or, when associated with others, took part in 5,287 arrests. That's true, isn't it?

A. That's true, yes.

Q. Okay. Now, what were you wearing that day?

A. I was wearing clothes.

Q. Shocking.

A. Yes, it is.

The "Condemned Penis" and Violated Husky

(Michael Chaney, Los Angeles)

[*From a Police Report*]: The Detective reported that he spoke with the reporting witness at great length and was apprised that the Uncle placed a condemn on his penis and performed sexual acts on the female dog, the Husky. The dog was yelping during the time of this incident. The Detective is investigating the family and will be conducting an investigation with regards to the dog. This is for Lude and Lascivious Acts with an Adult.

"Toughest Judge on the Tenth Circuit."

{ 9 }

Sentencing

The philosopher-lawyer Jeremy Bentham characterized as "dog law'"a system in which a person has no way of knowing that he is doing something wrong until he is punished for it.

LEONI V. STATE BAR, 39 CAL.3D 609, 629 (1985)
(GRODIN, J., CONCURRING AND DISSENTING)

Professor Coffee has noted the dilemma presented in seeking to sentence a corporation: "In the thirteenth century Pope Innocent IV forbade the practice of excommunicating corporations on the unassailable logic that, since the corporation had no soul, it could not lose one. He thus became the first legal realist."

JOHN COFFEE, JR., "NO SOUL TO DAMN;
NO BODY TO KICK," 79 MICH. L. REV. 386 N.2 (1981)

In what might serve as a monument to our Byzantine sentencing law . . . we are called upon to decide how many lifetimes a defendant can be sentenced to spend in prison based upon a plea agreement calling for him to spend only one. We hold that where a criminal defendant enters a guilty plea on the understanding that he will serve one lifetime in prison, he cannot be sentenced to serve two or more lifetimes without first being given an opportunity to withdraw his plea. By granting the defendant only one life, nature provides an absolute invulnerability to such supernumerary sentences.

PEOPLE V. KIM, 193 CAL.APP.4TH 1355, 1358 (2011)

Probation Report

(Delgado Smith, Texarkana, TX)

SCARS & TATTOOS: Scars: none; Tattoos: both arms, chest & back. The head of the defendant's penis is tattooed with a happy face.

Another Probation Report

(Arlin Armstrong)

The defendant offered the following written statement as part of his probation application:

> I didn't do the crime I was found guilty of. That's why I think I should be entitled to probation. So I can prove my innocence. I am currently having my lawyer filing papers to appeal my conviction. I was not a felon before being convicted of this crime. I don't feel I'm a felon now. I feel that I have been railroaded. The lawyer didn't take the right step in defending me. To say the least, I feel like shit.

Time Credits: Real and Imagined

(Samuel K. Eaton, Jr., Santa Barbara)

THE COURT Probation is revoked, and shall we do that then—
COUNSEL We can do that now. Because the deal was, the agreement was that the defendant is going to receive ninety days that's remaining on that with credit from September 19—
THE COURT How many days?
COUNSEL That is an actual seventeen plus—
THE COURT Ninety days. He's going to have seventeen actuals plus eight pretend which gives us twenty-five total.

Sentence Inflation California Style

(David McNeil Morse, San Francisco)

DA So the total that the People are recommending is 1,210 years before the defendant is eligible for parole, and after . . . he serves that, then it would be 22 consecutive life sentences.

Inmate Progress Report

(Suzanne Kingsbury, South Lake Tahoe)

Attached, please find records for the defendant. Note that for continuation high school period attendance accounting purposes T = there (in attendance) and A = absent. We are noting that there is a running battle between T and A. Currently the "A's" are winning over the "T's" 73 to 62. The "A's" have been on a roll for the month of October. In his first two years of high school he earned 3 credits. At his current rate of progress (1.5 credits per year), we estimate that it will take 146 2/3 years to graduate. His age at that time would be approximately 171 in the year AD 2136.

Letter of Recommendation

(Hon. Tim Murphy, Los Angeles)

Dear Judge,

I'm writing to you regarding my fiancé. I have decided that I am getting tired of the Court's bullshit. He told me to write you two to three letters a week. So I have been doing that with no response so far. My fiancé is a good person. He did a lot of drugs and was going out with that fourteen-year-old girl before he went in, but he has changed. He tells me how much he has changed whenever he calls me. I know that he will be fine once he gets out. He told me that he will only do drugs one time more and that is the night he gets out. After that, he will never do them again.

I am kinda scared sometimes, though. Because he threatens to kill everyone when he gets out. He gets so mad at the world and at me. But I still love him. He also told me that he might kill himself if he is locked up any longer. Please help us by letting him out early. I think that will stop him from hurting himself. And if he ever did hurt himself, I would hold you responsible. Because you are the person that put him in prison in the first place. I will do anything to help him get out early. Please let me know what I can do.

Probation Report Preliminaries

(Charles Weisselberg, Berkeley)

The probation officer met with the interpreter, who is, apparently, related to one of the intended victims. The interview was conducted at the jail where the defendant is incarcerated. The interpreter assured the probation officer that the defendant should be considered a hero in the Assyrian community because the victim is an insignificant opportunist who cares for nothing but to have his name exalted and to gain power and prestige from this incident. Another victim, on the other hand, is a Kurdish traitor deserving death and mutilation. The interpreter assured this writer that if he were standing before him today, the interpreter would kill him and "drink his blood." With these preliminaries established, the interview was conducted.

U.S. v. Polanco, 37 F.Supp.2d 262, 263 (SDNY 1999)

(Delgado Smith, Texarkana, TX)

The federal sentencing guidelines are like a Victorian corset around the body of lady justice. Its complicated design of laces, braces, buckles and bows make it devilishly difficult to put on and even more difficult to undo. Though it comes in a range of sizes, none of them feels right. Worst of all, its rigid stays that are supposed to shape justice, in whatever form is fashionable, so pinch and distort her natural contours as to cause permanent damage to her health.

Probation Evaluation

(Richard Krech, Oakland)

The defendant is suitable and eligible for probation. He views himself as an "ethical" drug dealer and drug user. He is proud of the fact that he usually holds a job and that he does not steal or commit acts of violence. During the interview he spoke of himself and some of his friends as "spoiled middle class kids" who are "dissatisfied with life." We found him to be intelligent and pleasant, but also someone who is not ready to change a lifestyle he has been in for well over twenty years.

Cat Burglar Identified

(Ruth Spear, Berkeley)

Regarding count 3: between March 8th and 9th, the victim reported that his car was broken into and reports a loss of an $800 amplifier and a $200 amplifier. Police dusted for fingerprints and removed the paw print which, after close review, examination and comparison, was positively identified as the minor's.

Discharge at Sentencing

(Dorothy Bischoff, San Francisco)

PROSECUTOR What does it take to get somebody sentenced
    to state prison in this city?
THE COURT Wait, wait, wait. I'm not going to allow that to
    go unanswered. You put me in a corner, miss.
PROSECUTOR Let me come up punching.
THE COURT Do you know what it takes? It takes honest, deli-

cate representation by the District Attorney's Office. It requires a district attorney who doesn't ask for state prison on every single case. It requires the person who is earnest and sensitive to issues. For you to stand here and ask that an eighteen-year-old boy without a record, with a family, a graduate of a high school who wants to go to college, and to ask that this man who had the indiscretion of having a weapon and negligently discharging it, where the victim, who has a right and has been notified by the probation department to come here and indicate whether this man should go to state prison—no victims have come here, although by statute they're required to come here. And for you to stand here and say that this man should be thrown away—and you say at least for two years, so you're saying six years—to me gives me a chance now to declare a recess, go to my bathroom and decide whether I want to vomit. Thank you.

Probation Interview

(John Crouch, Victorville)

[Per the defendant] I was at the sheriff's department to report that I was being harassed. I got arrested at the sheriff's office. The sheriff's officer lied and said that he had stopped me sometime earlier on a motorcycle and found drugs. He lied about stopping me and he lied about the drugs and the motorcycle and he lied and said that he found drugs on me. I was under the influence of drugs while I was at the sheriff's station. But that was because my attorney came into the room to interview me with an interpreter and they used some kind of gas on me. They drugged me. I was very bad from it. After they drugged me, they forced me to sign a plea bargain. The judge

asked me if I was under the influence and I told him that I wasn't. Even [the prosecutor] who was in court at that time noticed that I was under the influence and saw that there was something wrong with me. She told the Court that I was under the influence. I tried to explain to the judge that my attorney and the interpreter had gassed me but I don't think that they believed me.

Probation Report: Health of Defendant

(Ed Schulman, Los Angeles)

Defendant states that he is in a lot of pain from the gunshot wounds he suffered in the present offense. His left arm is permanently disabled. He received three gunshot wounds in the stomach, one gunshot wound in the upper chest, three gunshot wounds in the back, and four gunshot wounds in the right leg. He also received two gunshot wounds in the left arm. Otherwise he is healthy.

Probation Report: Bad Experience

(Richard Krech, Oakland)

The defendant describes the worst trauma he has experienced in the present case resulted during his trial testimony when his attorney repeatedly questioned him about his prior criminal record.

Probation Report: Defendant's Ability to Live in Oroville Without Committing Too Many Felonies

(Jerry Kenkel, Chico)

The defendant noted in talking to this officer that an unusual circumstance in his life that the Court might consider as an alternative to prison is that he has spent thirty years in Oroville, and with his family background, has not been convicted on a felony until now. During interview, this officer noted that the defendant, when discussing his innocence in various offenses, would exhibit facial jerkings and twitchings unlike at any other time of discussion.

Joining the Crowd

(Melissa K. Nappan, Sacramento)

The defendant attended Cloverdale High School. His education was interrupted when he was committed to juvenile hall for "being an asshole." He subsequently earned his GED.

Ignoring Pro-Social Lifestyle

[*U.S. v. Filipiak*, 466 F.3d 582, 584 (7th Cir. 2006)]

Filipiak also contends that the district judge did not consider her "pro-social lifestyle" (whatever in the world that means) in fashioning her sentence.

Fireworks at Sentencing

(Dennis Roberts, Oakland)

DA Defense Counsel's efforts and comments aside, I do not believe this Court can go any lower than the People have indicated in their sentencing memorandum, which is thirty years to life, without coming into disagreement with the clear intent of the Legislature and the letter of the law as set forth in the statutes. With regard to responding to Defense Counsel's multitude of other comments, I only have a couple of thoughts. I do not appreciate him getting up in open court and telling the family of the defendant that somehow I am responsible for their son going home in a box. I do not appreciate him implying that responsibility onto this Court. It is his client and his client alone who should be held accountable for his circumstances as they are right now. Neither I nor this Court nor the victim has done anything to put his client into the position that he's in. His client was the one that chose to get drunk. His client was the one that chose to carry that gun to the apartment that night. His client was the one that broke out those windows and initiated a fight. His client chose to draw that weapon and fire it into the victim. To lay blame on anyone else is completely improper and misleads the family members and this Court, and I take offense to it. Given the history of this case, violence that has already fallen upon the victim at the hands of this family, I think it is incredibly irresponsible of any counsel to get up and make comments like that.

DEFENSE COUNSEL I stand by every word I have spoken in this Court. I can't help the thin skin of a prosecutor any more than I can help the thin skin of the guards who put the Jews in concentration camps and gassed them because they were just doing their job as well. Maybe, I have a higher moral standard and I hold people to it, but to sit here and say it is not my fault, it is his fault. It is absolutely his fault. He knew the victim was a lying sack of garbage.

DA I am not going to listen to this.

COUNSEL Then go home and talk to your mommy about what a nasty guy you are dealing with. Tell her to give me a call.

THE COURT For the record, the DA has left the courtroom.

Not Nottingham Material

[*U.S. v. Repking*, 467 F.3d 1091,1096 (7th Cir. 2006)]

As we said at oral argument, we leave open the possibility that a one-day sentence of imprisonment might be justifiable for a defendant who rivals Robin Hood; but Repking, a millionaire who stole for himself and his friends, is not that defendant.

Probation Interview with the Lovely Interpreter

(Jack Campbell, San Diego)

It should be noted that at the beginning of the interview the defendant was staring at the interpreter's legs and the first couple of questions had to be repeated as he did not seem to be paying attention to what she was saying. He had to be told to concentrate on what she was saying and look at the probation officer. Several times during the interview this officer observed the defendant touching his scrotum.

It's Not My Fault

(Ken Quigley, San Francisco)

[*Defendant's statement to the probation officer*]

I'm a drug addict and alcoholic and don't remember dates. I didn't report because of you. You made me lose my job. Bitch!

"No further questions for this witness, Your Honor."

{ 10 }

The Witnesses

I went to Zimbabwe. I know how white people feel in America now;
relaxed! 'Cause when I heard the police car
I knew they weren't coming after me!

RICHARD PRYOR

I've been charged with murder for killing a man with sandpaper.
To be honest I only intended to rough him up a bit.

ANON

How Close Were You?

(John Henry Hingson, Oregon City, OR)

A. From eight or nine feet I could hear a belch, I could hear a fart.

Q. Have you ever heard me belch in here today?

A. I haven't directed my attention. That's not my role here to monitor you. I'm trying to make this impersonal.

That's a Definite Maybe

(Kate Hill-Germond, Princeton, NJ)

Q. Did anyone ever suggest to you that you change your testimony?

A. No.

Q. Is your testimony here today that you bought this beer at the Moran Hotel in Muncy?

A. Right.

Q. And you're absolutely sure about that?

A. I ain't positive. I ain't exactly positive. But I'm sure.

Money in the Bag

(Madeline McDowell, Lompoc)

On June 30, 2005, at about eight-twenty in the evening, Mr. F. was working alone at the Chevron gas station when a robber walks in, puts a gun on the counter and tells him to give him all the money. Mr. F. was so stunned when the robber told him to put

the money in the bag, he asked, "Paper or plastic?" The robber
replied, "Any bag, you motherfucker."

Mother Knows Best

(George Schraer, San Diego)

Q. Did you stop and talk to your son about what had occurred
outside?

A. Yes, I did. I asked him what was going on.

Q. Did your son respond?

A. Yes, he did.

Q. What did your son tell you happened outside that gate?

A. He said, it's just somebody shooting off firecrackers,
Mom.

Q. What did you respond?

A. I responded, firecrackers, my ass. That was a gun. It was a
.22 or a .25.

An Early Screamer

(Melissa Nappan, Sacramento)

Q. Did she use drugs?

A. I have read in a report that a neighbor in her apartment
complex has heard her screaming at her infant.

Q. That is of concern to you?

A. Yes, that is of concern.

Q. Why?

A. Because most parents don't scream at their infants. They

wait until they are three or four years old before they start
screaming at them.

Somebody Turned the Lights Out

(Kenneth R. Elliott, Oceanside)

Q. Actually, my original question was, if I ask you, did you
use methamphetamine today? Now, what does the word
"today" mean to you?

A. Today is when it gets light out.

Q. Okay. So let's say it's six-thirty tonight when it's dark.
That isn't today anymore?

A. No. It's the same day because it just continues on from
when it gets dark until the next light.

Q. Okay.

A. It's the same day.

Q. So it—day means daylight hours?

A. No, daylight is tomorrow until the next day when there's
light again.

Suitable Question

(John Henry Hingson, Oregon City, OR)

Q. Could you tell from his clothing what he did for a living?

A. You know sometimes you can tell . . . doctors wear their
doctor clothes and lawyers wear their law suits.

Abating a Lawsuit

(Matthew Ross, Forest Hills, NY)

[*In a landlord-tenant dispute where the husband and wife tenants sought an abatement in rent for alleged lousy apartment conditions*]

Q. Did you use the shower in the apartment?

TENANT Yes.

Q. Did you sleep in the apartment?

TENANT Yes.

Q. Did you cook in the apartment?

TENANT Yes.

HUSBAND Objection.

THE COURT What's the basis?

HUSBAND My wife is losing my case for me.

History's Royal Hand

(George Schraer, San Diego)

Q. And there are numerous people that have had contact with that item, the rape kit?

A. I wouldn't use the word "numerous."

Q. Four? Five?

A. Well, there's obviously the original medical technician that took it, myself, the criminal lab.

Q. Three.

A. And our storage area.

Q. Four.

A. And then transportation to Forensic Analytical.

Q. Five.

A. And then Forensic Analytical.

Q. Six. Are we getting a little bit toward numerous? We're getting more than a handful.

A. I would not have used the word "numerous." That's your word.

Q. Fine. It's more than you can count on one hand, isn't it?

THE COURT Only if you're not Anne Boleyn.

Hogging the Bed

(Katherine Houston, Ukiah)

Q. Can you describe the bedroom you found?

A. There was a bed, there was clutter in the bedroom, a large 350-pound pig in the bedroom. And basically, that's about it.

Q. What size bed was in there?

A. What size bed? I would say at least a queen size, maybe king size bed. There was rather a large clutter of items in the bedroom.

Q. Did it appear that the pig that you found in there had like a sleeping space or a bedroom area in there?

A. Yes.

Q. Were there items of clothing in that bedroom?

A. For the pig?

Q. No, not for the pig. For people. Well, for the pig, too.

Splendor in the Grass

(Carl M. Hancock, San Diego)

COUNSEL Did you see where one of the men's wallets fell?

WITNESS Yes.

Q. And where did it fall?

A. In, like, the—well, I think it was, like, in the—well in the grass, because—well, it's, like, the sidewalk, then like a little wall, there isn't really grass, but you can see grass in the grass.

Funny Break

(Susan Olson, Ventura)

Q. Did the nurse tell you whether or not her arm had been broken?

A. She pointed to the X-ray film where she indicated the break was, and stated that the name of the bone is the humorous bone.

Shape of Things

(Robert Derham, San Francisco)

Q. Did you ever talk to the detective about a person named Dickhead?

A. I might have.

Q. Did you ever tell them that Dickhead was there packaging the dope on the day of the murder?

A. I don't remember that.

Q. Did you ever tell him that you had talked to Dickhead about buying some dope or trying to work out the deal in the first place?

A. Yes, but I never talked to Dickhead.

Q. Do you know who Dickhead is?

A. Yes.

Q. What is his name?

A. What is his name?

Q. Yes.

A. Dickhead.

Q. Is that his real name?

A. I don't know his real name.

Q. Is that a nickname?

A. Yes.

Q. Is that based on the appearance of his head?

Clintonian Speed

(Paul Geragos, Los Angeles)

WITNESS Well, I have a twenty-year-old son. I can't remember when I went to bed with his father at this date either. I'd have to look back at my records for that. Just thirty incidents with this gentleman that sex wasn't to have anything to do with being killed. This is nerve-wracking on me.

Q. I understand. I'm going to try not to wrack your nerves, but I do need to ask you some questions. So you mentioned an intimate relationship with the defendant.

A. Like I said, we went out on a date. We kissed. I didn't go to bed with him until the second date. That was sex. That wasn't a love party.

Q. But just so I'm clear, you remained the night on his boat; isn't that correct?

A. No. He was on my boat.

Q. I see. And after that, that first time where you engaged in sex with the defendant, did you continue to have a sexual relationship with him for some period of time?

A. No. Because he came so quick and I guess . . .

THE COURT You've answered.

WITNESS Sex wasn't good with him, so I didn't continue to have a sexual relationship with him. Let's put it that way.

Q. Your testimony is that you had sex with him one time, that was all?

A. I had sex with him on one occasion. I didn't say one time.

Q. No more sexual contact with the defendant after that?

A. Do you consider kissing or hugging or talking sexual contact?

COUNSEL [to Court] Sounds familiar, doesn't it?

THE COURT The Clinton definition?

WITNESS Yeah. That was just the sex thing for me. He wasn't up to my goals or however you say it. I wasn't interested.

Contempt in the Digital Age

(John Kucera, Redding)

Order of Contempt:

On the conclusion of the hearing, contemner arose from his seat in the back row of the courtroom, and began walking forward in order to leave the courtroom. Persons exiting the courtroom from the back row must walk forward and make a right turn in order to leave by the side door. As contemner was beginning to turn right, he came to a complete stop, turned to face this bench officer who was presiding from the bench, made eye contact with the Court, and raised his right hand upward until the hand was raised in front of his face and simultaneously lowered all but the middle finger which remained extended upward in what is commonly known as "the finger" or legally as the *digitus impudicus*. Contemner maintained eye contact with me throughout the exhibition of the "rude finger."

[Contemner fined $315]

Close Enough

(Richard Schaffer, Stockton)

THE COURT Mr. Defendant, would you stand, please.

COUNSEL Mr. Witness, now that you viewed the defendant standing up, how does his height compare to the individual running out that evening?

A. I would say it was about 30 yards away. I guess—it was about six feet. I don't know how tall he is. But that's about it.

Q. Is his height similar to the individual's that evening?

A. Give or take probably a foot.

Quackery

(John Henry Hingson, Oregon City, OR)

Q. You mentioned that you saw the defendant order straight shots?

A. Yes, I did.

Q. A round of straight shots?

A. A round of six straight shots.

Q. But you said he put it on somebody else's bill?

A. On Rob's tab.

Q. So as far as you saw, the defendant wasn't even paying for his own drinks?

A. That round. That's the only one I saw him order.

Q. That's the only one you saw him order?

A. Yes.

Q. Was it one of those drinks, one of those straight shots that you saw him drink?

A. No.

Q. It was something outside of those six?

A. Something different.

Q. What was it that you saw him drink, do you know?

A. It was like a B-52, like a triple-layer drink, a B-52 or duck fart.

Q. That's a new one on me.

COUNSEL What was that last one?

DA B-52 or duck fart.

WITNESS A duck fart.

Q. And what are those? Are you familiar with what those are?

A. I don't know what's in it.

COUNSEL I object to the competence of the witness.

Q & A

(J. Converse Bright, Valdosta, GA)

Q. My name is Hicks. I'm an attorney. I represent Vincent.

A. I'm Grandison. I'm a convict thanks to Vincent. All right?

Clarification

(Steven D. Powell, Ventura)

Q. Who taught you that term, "oral copulation"?

A. Steve.

Q. Who?

A. My attorney.

Q. You're referring to the deputy district attorney seated at counsel table?

A. He taught you that term?

Q. He didn't teach me—he taught me that term, that word, another name for giving head, whatever. But he didn't teach me how to do it.

Total Recall

(Charles Robinson, Redwood City)

Q. At a later time, did you recall something about the murder weapon, and what Tim had said?

A. Yes.

Q. What did you recall?

A. Tim didn't like Joe, and so he said that Joe deserved to be beaten with a bat.

Q. When did he say that?

A. I don't know when he said that. I think it was the time coming back from Disneyland.

Q. When did you remember that?

A. I remembered it last week. I woke up in the middle of the night and I remembered it. I didn't think it was a big deal, so I went to sleep. I told myself not to think about it. I went back to sleep.

Q. So that would have been before the conversation with Tim?

A. Right, but I didn't remember that I remembered that. I remember, I remember when Tim brought this up I remember thinking, would I remember this? And now I don't remember it anymore. So I tried to remember it again.

Q. Did you tell Shelly about any baseball bat?

A. No, I did not tell her about the baseball bat.

Q. Was it in another dream that you had on Thursday night that you remembered a baseball bat?

A. No, I had remembered the baseball bat, I believe, when I

did remember that—let's see. I remembered the baseball bat. I remembered the baseball bat being brought up. I remember, I remember Tim saying it and I remember remembering it, like, three in the morning. And then I remember forgetting it and then I remembered remembering it again. And I don't remember on when I remembered again. I remember forgetting it because I did not want to remember it and then I remember remembering it again.

'Roid Rage

(Paul Fromson, Merced)

Q. Did you receive any injury from the gun going off?
A. No.
Q. Didn't receive any pain at all?
A. No.
Q. Any numbing or anything like that?
A. No.
Q. You didn't have any injuries on you from this alleged struggle?
A. No.
Q. You weren't injured in any way during this time?
A. Other than having a real bad case of the hemorrhoids.

Marital Medicine

(Richard Krech, Oakland)

Q. What kind of medication are you on?
A. I had a Triavil. I do 100 milligrams. I have to take them three times a day.

Q. What is the medication again?

A. Triavil and Cogentin.

Q. What is that for?

A. For my marriage because I had a nervous breakdown.

Little Head

(Larry Gibbs, Berkeley)

Q. Who was it that was with you doing the robberies?

A. One of my so-called friends. Just an associate.

Q. An associate?

A. Yeah.

Q. Well, who was it?

A. His name is Little Head Jessie. That's what we call him, but I don't know his name, his real name.

Q. You don't know his name?

A. That's his street name.

Q. Why do people call that fellow Little Head?

A. Because his head's little.

Saturday Night Live Court

(Kim Malcheski, San Francisco)

Q. What did the girl that owns the apartment look like?

A. She's blond and skinny; real pretty girl.

Q. Real pretty? Okay.

A. Like a ho.

Q. Like a ho?

A. A ho, you know, like a bitch.

Q. Oh. You mean, like a whore?

A. Yeah.

Momma

(Mark Arnold, Bakersfield)

Q. And did you ask her if she had had a sexual relationship with the defendant?

A. Yes, I did.

Q. And what aid she tell you in that regard?

A. She told me that they had had a sexual relationship for approximately one month. And that the reason she had the sexual relationship was that her mother had been a slut and that was her role model; and, therefore, she had become a slut.

Clearing the Air

(John Y. Lee, Los Angeles)

Q. What did he specifically do? I am sorry. Did he place his buttocks on top of your face?

A. No. He just like squatted down over me and just farted and got up. Then they are saying, "We are going to give the boy a blanket party, ought to shove his toilet in the head and drown him."

COUNSEL For the record, I think "fart" is flatulate.

THE COURT If you want to testify, we will swear you in. Other than that, if you want further explanation on that, you can do that on cross.

Q. At the point where he had farted, you want to clarify for Counsel what that means?

A. Yes. That means flatulated.

Q. In simple English, he released bad air from his buttocks?

A. Exactly.

One for the Road

(Michael Thorman, Hayward)

Q. Had you consumed any alcohol on the day that you were shot?

A. Yeah.

Q. What type of alcohol had you consumed?

A. Budweiser. I drank a beer after Kenny shot me. I asked him if I could have a beer. I grabbed a beer and I was drinking a beer, waiting to die.

Q. Okay. So you had a beer after you were shot?

A. Yes, sir.

Q. Just one?

A. Yes, sir.

Q. How many beers had you had before you were shot?

A. I drank about a six-pack a day. A six-pack or twelve-pack, depending on how long the day is going to last.

Jesus Lives in Oak Park

(John Cotter, Sacramento)

Q. When did you leave?

A. That same night.

Q. What time?

A. About ten or eleven.

Q. And where did you go?

A. To my friend's house.

Q. And you stayed overnight there, I guess?

A. Yes.

Q. Who is your friend?

A. Jesus.

COUNSEL Object as relevancy.

THE COURT The objection is overruled.

WITNESS My friend is Jesus.

Q. Where does he live?

A. In Oak Park.

Magna Est Veritas

(David P. Carleton, Los Angeles)

THE COURT I had observed this witness approach the witness stand. Is he sober? He appears to me to be intoxicated. I noticed the lady who's seated back there, the young attractive lady, she's like instructing him, like "sit up," "sit up." Is he sober?

DA I would say that I'm not qualified to answer that question. The woman in the front row is his daughter. When I talked to him briefly, he appeared to answer the questions in a responsive manner.

THE COURT Did you detect any odor of alcohol on his breath?

DA Yes, I did. I think that Defense Counsel can perhaps bring that up. However, I don't think it disqualifies him as a witness.

THE COURT Well, wait a minute. Of course they say *in vino veritas*, "In wine there's the truth," a lot of people, when they drink, tell the truth for the first time in their life. What do you think?

DEFENSE COUNSEL I'm wondering if the Court is going to inquire whether he's going to share it or not.

THE COURT We can try.

Lawyer Billing the Client

(Delgado Smith, Texarkana, TX)

COUNSEL And not only that, Judge, there is a great yiddish word called *chutzpah*. Here is a great example of it. Not only did they refuse to release to him his own tax papers, not only did they refuse to talk to him or his lawyers because they were talking to the prosecution, okay, they billed him $32,000 for the time they spent. I know even the prosecutor is shocked. Unbelievable. They billed him for the time they spent ratting on their client with the district attorneys. I couldn't believe it.

THE COURT Is that like saying they have a lot of *huevos*?

COUNSEL *Mucho huevos granditos.*

Polite Witness Meets the Judge

(Delgado Smith, Texarkana, TX)

A. If I could draw a diagram.

THE COURT Yes.

A. Thank you, Your Honor.

THE COURT For what, sir?

A. For allowing me to explain myself.

THE COURT I don't mean to seem rude, but I want you to just confine to listening to the questions and answering them and not adding editorial comments or unnecessary thanks.

A. Thank you.

Feelings

(A. J. Kutchins, Berkeley)

Q. This gun, where was it pointing?

A. Probably at the chest area.

Q. Whose chest area?

A. Mine.

Q. How close to your chest area was the gun pointing?

A. Probably like four feet.

Q. And so the barrel was pointed directly at your chest?

A. Yeah.

Q. How were you feeling at this time?

A. Vulnerable.

Family Court: Dangerous Place to Be

(David McGlaughlin, Philadelphia)

THE COURT Why haven't you paid your child support?

A. I got fired.

Q. What was your last employment?

A. Philadelphia Police Department.

Q. We don't like people to get fired when they have children.

COUNSEL I have a record that he resigned.

THE COURT You're under oath. Did you resign or were you fired?

A. I was forced to resign. That's a firing in my book.

Q. Please don't play games with me. Were you fired or did you resign?

A. I was forced to resign. I was fired. Call personnel. I had no choice.

Q. I'm not going to call anybody. I want to know what you're going to do about these kids.

A. As soon as I get a job. I've been looking for the last two months.

COUNSEL It's the second time he has resigned from the police force and his obligation to support these three children.

A. How am I going to support myself if I get fired?

THE COURT They'll support you at the county prison.

A. Oh, thank you. That's going to help a lot, Your Honor.

Q. It won't hurt your children. You're not supporting them.

A. In other words, I'm being punished twice. I got fired from my job, locked up, and you're going to punish me for the same thing? *[At this point, he struck and kicked his wife]* Send me to jail for that, cocksucker. *[To wife]* Die, you bitch. . . .

THE COURT Let the record reflect the defendant assaulted his wife. He is sentenced to six months in the House of Correction for contempt, and a warrant is to be sworn out for this assault. Go with the Sheriff.

A. I'll kill her, fucking bitch.

THE COURT Get out of here. . . . A warrant should be sworn for this assault. I'm willing to be a witness. Put me down as a witness.

"And Wretches Hang That Jurymen May Dine"

(David J. Briggs, Martinez)

Q. You assisted in the collection of gunshot residue evidence?

A. Yes.

Q. In what way?

DA Objection, irrelevant.

THE COURT Sustained.

COUNSEL She described her crime scene investigation and this comes within the scope of that testimony.

DA What's the relevance?

THE COURT I'm trying to get her out of here before lunch.

Hawaii 5 Oh Oh

(Richard Krech, Oakland)

Q. And you walked outside with your boyfriend and the child?

A. Yes, the children.

Q. And you tried to get into the car that was parked in front of your apartment?

A. Right.

Q. What happened when you tried to get into it? They pulled a *Hawaii 5-0*. Halt, that kind of thing?

THE COURT Would you explain what happened? I'm not sure we all agree what a *Hawaii 5-0* is. So what did happen?

A. The police came out of the bushes and came out of everywhere, basically, and told me and my children to put our hands on the car and freeze and don't move and they slammed my boyfriend on the ground. I guess they thought he was the person they were looking for.

Q. Like on *Hawaii 5-0*.

A. Right.

Witness for the Prosecution

(Kim Dodge, South Lake Tahoe)

Q. Miss, did you ever give this defendant permission to take the bag from the store?

A. Not that I know of. This is the hard part.

Q. Why don't you tell us about what happened then?

A. It has something to do with drugs. I've never been on drugs myself. I think he [defendant] believed I wanted him to take the money. I heard a tape go off, and it was close to my voice. It sounded like my voice. It was probably somebody else's voice and that voice was saying that he should take the money, so I think he thinks that I wanted him to take the money.

Q. Where was this tape playing?

A. I don't know. I just heard it. It has some bearing on the case. I know it happened a long time ago if it happened at all. See, I was attacked in my sleep and I was brainstormed and sometimes I wrote songs and poetry and all this. And nobody ever believed me because they referred it to mental health.

Q. Are you saying that you in your own mind heard some voices that sounded like you indicated that he could take the money?

A. Yes.

Q. Did he hear that?

A. I don't know. But I thought I'd tell you to give him, you know, a fair chance because these are underground activities and I have no control over them. It's possible he heard it too.

[Motion to dismiss granted, after which the Court addresses the defendant]

THE COURT Let me caution you, sir, there's no question in my mind that you are just about as whacko as she is. If you mess up in this town, then it's adios.

COUNSEL He's going to another county. He has a prelim waiting for him on destruction of county jail property.

THE COURT There is a God!

On Talking to God While out of Body During a Robbery

(Michael Thorman, Hayward)

Q. You're looking at this point, the top of the head of some-body who's robbing the bank?

A. Kind of the side. Yeah, kind of the side, top.

Q. Got a profile look?

A. Yes.

Q. And you told us there is a point in time when you're say-ing, "Excuse me, sir, there's no wall. What do you want me to do?" Was that before or after your out-of-body experience?

A. That was before.

Q. And by the time this out-of-body experience ended, had the suspect gone back behind the teller line here?

A. No, he did not.

Q. He was still there when you came back into your body?

A. That's correct.

Q. And this may be very difficult to answer, because I know that in terms of making an identification and looking at features, that it's a whole experience the whole time the person is there. Is part of your identification based on seeing this person while you're up above him, outside your body?

A. No, none of it.

Q. What's was going through your mind when you were up above the situation looking down?

A. I was having a little conversation with God, and I told him basically because I thought this minute that I was dead, that I had waited ten years to get married, which I was supposed to be doing in six days. And if You expected to see me in five minutes, You were going to have one ticked-off lady. So I told Him, "Please don't take this as a threat, but I'd be a little bit upset." So I'm not saying that He took that as a threat and put me back in my body, but it was a very quick conversation. I didn't see anybody in white robes or anything like that. It was a very smooth transition.

Q. You had out-of-body experiences before?

A. No.

Q. This was a onetime occurrence?

A. It was. I didn't even have one when I was on the floor in the home invasion.

Q. Okay. And probably because everybody wants to know, did the wedding happen six days later?

A. You better believe it.